I0769926

Legends of Lower Gods

MAXIMO D. RAMOS

PHOENIX PUBLISHING HOUSE
927 Quezon Avenue, Quezon City

Contents

Preface

A WIDE VARIETY of pre-Islamic and pre-Christian deities haunt the Philippine countryside. This explains why few of our village folk venture out after dark.

These pre-Spanish gods I have classified under twelve groups:

1. *Demons*—tall, dark, and ugly creatures that haunt large trees in or near human habitations.
2. *Dragons*—usually large animal forms such as pythons, crocodiles, and sharks that the folk avoid encountering. But they are often spoken to with awe or reverence and are thought to bring good fortune. Eclipses are thought to be caused by a huge sky dragon—the *laho* of the Tagalogs and Pampangos—swallowing the sun or moon. The folk believe that thunder is the sound coming out of the folds of the sky dragon's long body.
3. *Dwarfs*—old men who dwell underground with jars of treasure, entering and leaving their habitat through termite mounds on which they often invisibly sit and give itches and cast dust into the eyes of those who molest them.
4. *Elves*—short or tall fair-complexioned tree-dwelling legendary beings that try to seduce the men or women they fancy, steal rice and fish from kitchens

and fishtraps, and give treasure to those who please
them.
5. *Ghouls*—Aswang that devour corpses and are scared
off by bright light and loud noise around the dead.
6. *Giants*—relatively harmless large human and animal
forms that often interact with people.
7. *Merfolk*—fish-tailed men and women found in
rivers, bays, and seas but living in luxurious
dwellings to which they take the men or women
they capture.
8. *Ogres*—man-eating large creatures, usually in the
shape of ugly humans but in some cases of animals
and birds that devour people.
9. *Vampires*—pretty women aswang with long tubular
tongues through which they suck out blood from
their human victims, usually their dancing partners
in night spots.
10. *Viscera Takers*—good-looking women aswang with
enormously extendible tube tongues through which
they suck out the entrails or fetuses of their human
victims.
11. *Werebeasts*—aswang in the form of dogs or other
fierce Philippine animals that attack people at night,
devour them, and then resume their harmless
human form.
12. *Witches*—men and usually women aswang who
have the power to make people severely ill.

The beliefs in these twelve groups of demonological
beings have shaped Philippine culture and Philippine
behavior because the folk fear and try hard to propitiate
them or counteract the harm they do.

> Why tell of *tikbalang* and gnome
> To little ones at school—
> Of *kapre* in *balete* home
> And dwarf on *punso* stool?
>
> You think they care for long ago
> And tales of far away?

Why don't you tell of just-and-so
And deeds of men today?

Because the children's eyes must see,
The children's ears must hear
What quickens them to ecstasy,
What wakens them to fear.

How indigent some wordlings be
With all their hoard of gold.
How little known the treasury
The humble tale can hold.

—Maximo D. Ramos

MAXIMO D. RAMOS, the first editor in chief of Phoenix Publishing House, was associated with the company from 1963 until his death on December 12, 1988. As editor and consultant, he gathered together a team of teachers who were creative, understood the needs of Filipino students, knew their pedagogy, and, above all, were committed to the ideals of nationhood espoused by my father, Dr. Ernesto Y. Sibal.

The present leadership of Phoenix Publishing House in the textbook field in all subject areas on all three levels of the educational system is due, in a large measure, to the unfaltering loyalty and passion for work of Dr. Ramos.

Dr. Ramos never relaxed his own personal pursuit of the Muse and continued to write short stories, poems, and essays. At the same time, he devoted special attention to serious research on Philippine mythology and folklore. All these were done as he taught and performed administrative duties at the Philippine Normal College and later at the University of the East.

Phoenix Publishing House takes pride in publishing these ten volumes of the essential works of Dr. Ramos. We know that his legacy will fire the imagination of Filipino students and inspire them to know more about their own folkways and folklore and to write them down for others to enjoy and appreciate. Dr. Ramos's only limitation perhaps is access to Filipino language as medium of his literary output. But he has shown the Filipino student that one can master the English language and use it to advantage in portraying Philippine reality. And because the setting is Filipino and the experiences are part of the Filipino tradition, we know that his writings will appeal to children and to adults as well.

His works, collectively titled REALMS OF MYTHS AND REALITY, consist of the following:

    I.   TALES OF LONG AGO IN THE PHILIPPINES
   II.   PHILIPPINE MYTHS, LEGENDS, AND FOLKTALES
  III.   LEGENDS OF LOWER GODS
  IV.   THE CREATURES OF MIDNIGHT
   V.   THE ASWANG COMPLEX IN PHILIPPINE FOLKLORE
  VI.   PHILIPPINE DEMONOLOGICAL LEGENDS AND THEIR CULTURAL BEARINGS
 VII.   BOYHOOD IN MONSOON COUNTRY
VIII.   PATRICIA OF THE GREEN HILLS AND OTHER STORIES
  IX.   REMEMBRANCE OF LENTS PAST AND OTHER ESSAYS
   X.   THE CREATURES OF PHILIPPINE LOWER MYTHOLOGY

This collection is our tribute to Dr. Maximo D. Ramos and our contribution to Filipiniana.

J. ERNESTO SIBAL
Publisher

Demons

The Banana Jewel

A YOUTH WAS WALKING through a banana grove one dark night when he heard the squeak of a leafsheath directly overhead. He looked up and saw a banana blossom bend to earth under its own weight. As the heart-shaped blossom bent down, a glowing object dropped from it and started flitting about among the banana leaves like a sleepy butterfly among flowers.

Now the youth had often heard that the banana jewel, or *mutya*, dropped only from a banana flower bending toward the east in the middle of the night. It was said that whoever caught the jewel in his mouth and kept it there would become the strongest of men, but he who caught it and let it go again would become mad.

The youth had long wanted to test his courage and often wished he could see a banana jewel fall. He leaped up and caught the glowing jewel in his mouth. The jewel was cold like a stone and he tucked it against his cheek.

Instantly there was a heavy rustle in the thick banana grove. A dark giant grabbed him and lifted him into the air. The creature was tall and heavy, and its muscles bulged like the branch of an old tree.

But the man had gained his strength fast, for the power of the jewel in his mouth had surged into his

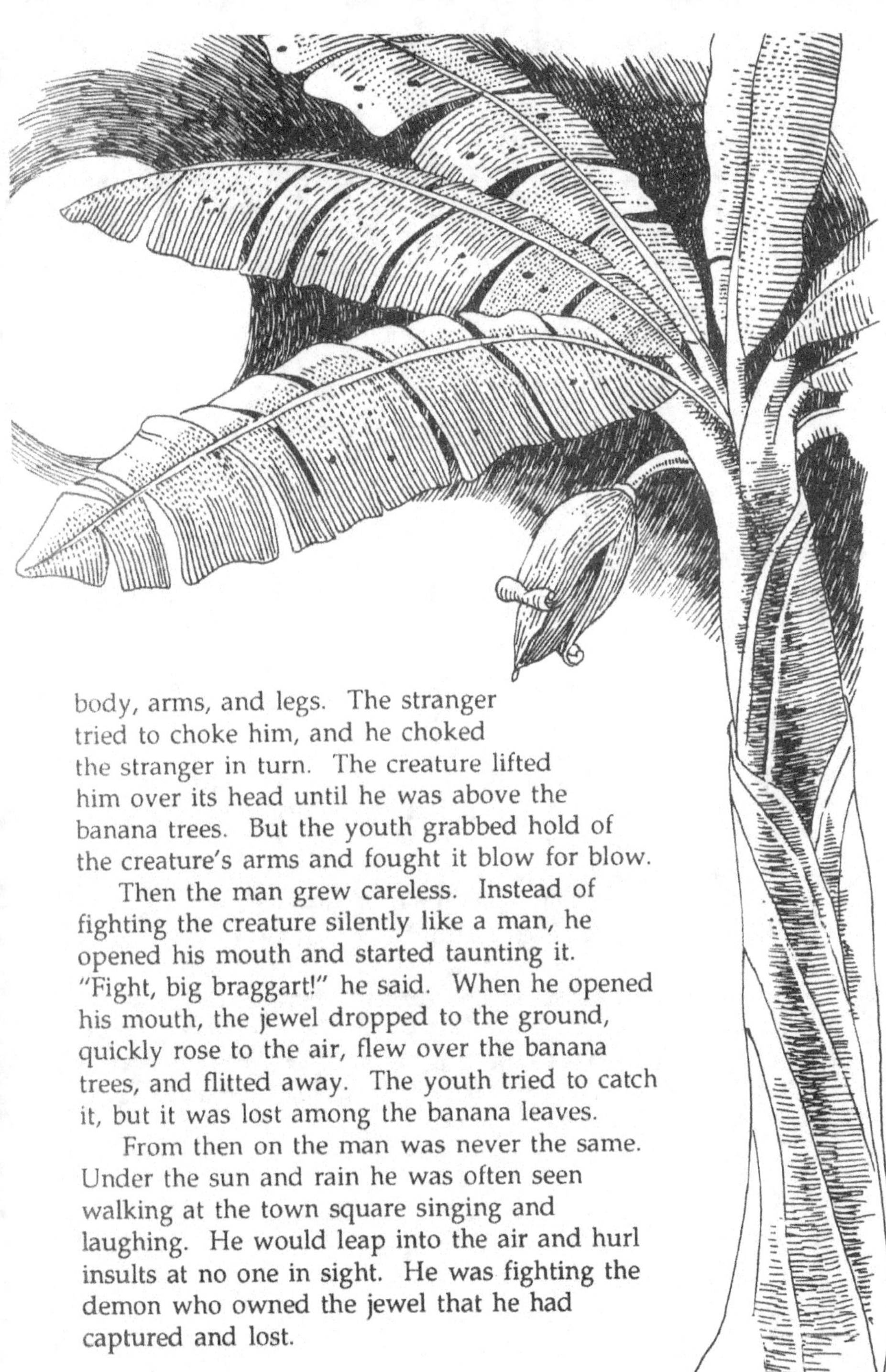

body, arms, and legs. The stranger
tried to choke him, and he choked
the stranger in turn. The creature lifted
him over its head until he was above the
banana trees. But the youth grabbed hold of
the creature's arms and fought it blow for blow.

Then the man grew careless. Instead of
fighting the creature silently like a man, he
opened his mouth and started taunting it.
"Fight, big braggart!" he said. When he opened
his mouth, the jewel dropped to the ground,
quickly rose to the air, flew over the banana
trees, and flitted away. The youth tried to catch
it, but it was lost among the banana leaves.

From then on the man was never the same.
Under the sun and rain he was often seen
walking at the town square singing and
laughing. He would leap into the air and hurl
insults at no one in sight. He was fighting the
demon who owned the jewel that he had
captured and lost.

Headless Creature

A BOY CAME HOME pale and panting. "Did the *pugot* try to get you?" his mother asked him jokingly. "Why are you so pale?"

"He had no head," he abruptly began. "He stood by a large tree beside the road. He ran after me but didn't get me."

His mother's eyes popped when she realized how near the truth her question had hit. "Was he big and dark?" she asked.

He nodded his head.

"Come home before sundown from now on," his father said. "It's lucky you didn't panic. If you had, you would have come home with an addled brain."

"Why didn't you tell me earlier?" complained the boy.

"Each man has to meet his demon," his grandfather replied. "You have met and survived your demon, and now you are a man."

The Boy and the Tikbalang

A FARMER'S LITTLE SON was hurrying home one night. He had run an errand to his uncle's house in the next clearing, but the rain did not stop till after sundown and so he started late.

A stranger overtook him under a dark *kalumpang* tree. The boy kept his eyes on the ground and tried not to look at him. But from the tail of his eye he saw that he was the tallest man he had ever seen. He had dark, long hair, his legs were thin, and his feet went clop-clop-clop along the stony trail.

"You are wet from the rain," said the stranger, keeping in step with the boy. "And aren't you a long way from home?"

"I'll get there after a few bends in the trail," replied the boy, his eyes on the stranger's feet.

He glanced up and saw a red glow from the stick in the stranger's mouth. How tall he was, and what a large mouth!

"Have you been walking long?" the stranger asked after a while.

The boy shook his head.

"You're sure you know the way now?" The stranger's voice was oddly high-pitched for such a large man.

"Yes, sir," replied the boy. "I have taken this trail many times before." He slackened his pace, hoping the stranger would go ahead and leave him. But the stranger kept in step with him. The boy glanced up again and saw that the stranger had no shirt on. His long black hair hung down to his shoulders and coarse hair grew on the back of his neck. His eyes glistened with blue flame and his large teeth shone.

"I could show you a shortcut if I knew where you live," said the stranger. "Who did you say your father was?"

"I don't tell my father's name to strangers," replied the boy and walked on in silence.

By and by the stranger tried to take the boy's hand, but the boy pulled it away. The stranger's hand was rough and cold.

Before long the boy realized that he had indeed lost his way. When the stranger took his hand again, he let him. The stranger's cigar glowed brighter as he turned from the trail toward taller and darker trees. "Come this way," he said.

They walked and walked. They paused and walked again, but they got no nearer his home. The boy felt exhausted and sat down to rest. When he closed his eyes, the creature picked him up in his arms and galloped deeper into the forest with him. The stranger had a strong goat smell which dizzied him.

The stranger put the boy down in the middle of a thick cluster of bamboo and left him there.

The boy cried, "Let me out! Let me out!" but the stranger's feet went clop-clop-clop and his high-pitched voice came "Heh-heh-heh!" and faded in the distance.

The boy cried and cried. He heard the fearful noises of the night in the woods and he cried louder. Then, tired out, he lay down and went to sleep.

It was morning when he woke up. With great difficulty he wormed his way through the bamboo thicket and got out at last. Kalumpang trees with foul-smelling blooms grew there.

He drank water from a little pool on the ground and ate wild fruit. Then he felt stronger and cried again.

Meanwhile, his parents waited all night for him to come home. They hurried to a brother's house and asked if he had not been there. He had. "We asked him to spend the night with us because it was drizzly, but he insisted on coming home," the brother said.

They hunted for him in the woods. "Imong!" they shouted. "We're here! Come!" They looked under the trees, and they looked under the shrubs and bushes. Then they looked in the river, calling, "Come out, Imong! We're here!"

Toward the end of the long day the boy heard them. He ran out and said, "Father! Mother! Uncle!"

His father took him in his arms. "You have a high fever, Son," he said and bore him home.

His mother gave him chicken broth and soft-boiled white rice and then put him to sleep. They watched over him, feeling his brow and shaking their heads as they whispered among themselves.

The boy woke up on the fifth day. His brow had grown cool and his eyelids were no longer heavy. "I met a tall man in the woods," he told them. "He said he would show me the way but I refused to go with him. I lost my way and followed him. We walked and walked. I grew too tired to walk on and sat down to rest. Then he picked me up and ran. He put me in a thick bamboo clump and left me there. I cried myself to sleep. I woke up in the morning and cried some more. Then I made my way out of the bamboo thicket. There was water to drink and wild fruit to eat. I stayed there because I didn't know where to go."

"Was the tall stranger thin?" his father asked.

The boy nodded.

"Had he a long face and did long hair grow on his neck?" his mother asked.

The boy nodded again. "He overtook me under a kalumpang tree," he said. "I was walking along and then he was suddenly beside me."

"And had he horse's feet and a horse's high-pitched voice?" asked his uncle.

The boy nodded.

"That was a *tikbalang* surely," said his father. "It is a demon that lives in large trees with large rounded leaves. It has the body and arms of a man but the head and hind legs of a horse. It made you lose your way and tried to frighten you. If you had been frightened, you would have become crazy. Then you wouldn't know what to do and what to say."

"Never, never go with a stranger in the woods again, Son," his mother said.

The Farmer and the Manhorse

In a village in Lian, Batangas, there lived a farmer so hardworking that he often left his fields for home long after sunset. He was fearless and nothing could daunt him.

One day, having done his tasks early, he went home just after sundown. He was following the narrow road villageward when, glancing at the wayside because he thought he heard a soft whinny, he saw a horselike man—or a manlike horse—seated on a rock. Its face was long and thin and a tuft of coarse hair drooped over its forehead. Its neck, long and thin, too, was ridged with an abundant growth of hair. Its arms were hairy but ended in human fingers, and its hind legs were so lanky that its knees hung well above its pricked ears. It was a creature known thereabouts as the tikbalang.

The farmer walked to the creature and said, "How is it with you?"

The tikbalang turned its large eyes to him but did not reply.

"Let's be friends even if we can't talk to each other," said the farmer, reaching out and amiably stroking its mane. As he did so, his fingers brushed off three strands of the creature's mane and he decided to keep them. "They will serve for slip snares for quails and

pigeons," he thought, putting them in his pocket and
proceeding home after bowing politely to the tikbalang.

He was on the same road a few nights later after
another hard day of threshing. He had left four sacks
inside his hut. When he was about to reach the rock on
which he met the tikbalang, he heard a clop-clop of
hoofs behind him. He turned and saw the tikbalang, on
its back his four sacks of rice expertly balanced.

The man expected the long-legged creature to come
abreast of him in a moment but it did not. So he
slowed down his steps, but the creature slowed down,
too. He walked faster and the tikbalang lengthened its
steps and fell back again when he slowed down. Then
he understood that the creature wanted to be his
follower, his slave and not his equal.

The tikbalang became his faithful beast of burden.
Before the next planting season it plowed his fields by
night and sowed the seed rice in a bed it made and
fenced off. When the seedlings were tall enough and
the rains came, the tikbalang plowed the fields anew
and harrowed them for the transplanting.

The man had a cart, and the tikbalang pulled it between farm and village well before dawn and after sunset so that the neighbors would not see it. When the rice was heavy in ear, the tikbalang came to reap the panicles at night, spread them out under the sky before the sun rose, and soon after nightfall gathered the grain and trampled the seeds off the panicles on the threshing floor in the middle of the field.

In a few seasons the farmer was rich and, contrary to what he had sometimes heard, he never paid his soul to the creature for its service.

The Black Demon

IN MAY a farmer at the forehead end of Luzon rose before dawn when there was a moon shining overhead. He wanted to do some plowing before the sun came up.

At one corner of the field stood a big mango tree, and when he looked, he thought he saw a branch of the tree swaying up and down although there was no breeze. He made several turns in the field with the plow, and each

time he came close to the tree and saw the branch
swaying, he wondered what made that one branch
sway up and down when everything else was still.

Then before the day broke, he looked closer and saw
the branch bend all the way to the ground.

Unafraid, for he was the strongest man in the valley
and had known this field since he could toddle over a
dike, he strode to the spot and came upon a little white
puppy with long, curly hair.

"Someone is going to miss his handsome little pet,"
he thought, picking up the puppy and walking back to
his plow with it. Then he decided he had done enough
plowing for the morning and thought he should
surprise his children with the handsome little animal.
He unhitched his carabao and let it loose to graze by
the river.

Then he looked at the pup again, and he gasped, for
it had grown much larger. It had turned into a
monstrous hound with eyes as large as his palms and
ears like gabi leaves. Then he realized that the beast's
legs were trailing on the ground.

He dropped the creature and whipped out his bolo.
But the creature made one long bound, landed on the
farther side of the river, and vanished in the shadows.

He deduced that a black demon, the pugot, lived in
the mango tree. For several mornings he smudged the
tree though it was laden with fruit and needed no
smudging. He burned leaves that exuded a strong
smell when burned, and in time the demon left the tree
for another and was never seen there again.

The Demon Tree

A CLUSTER OF LARGE TREES grew on a high bank over-looking the Cagayan River. Few people took shelter under those trees even when caught in a sudden rain, for it was said that a big black *kapre* lived in the largest of them. Fishermen who strayed into that part of the river by night came away with lisped accounts of a large black creature they saw standing under a tree.

The most common report was that the kapre was twelve feet tall and was often seen standing quietly under the tree or seated on one of its branches, its large feet almost touching the ground. The creature would grow shorter and shorter and then taller and taller. Sometimes a black carabao or boar with eyes as large as a man's palm and a mouth sending out a blue or green flame stood under the tree. Or the creature was headless and a weird flame could be seen leaping out of its open throat.

An old man who knew about these things said that the mysterious beasts were really different forms of the same demon, who changed its size and shape to terrify people and make them lose their wits. If a child passed by and saw the frightful creature, he would panic and run home screaming. He would continue screaming till he died.

Don Antonio had made a fortune in lumber and, passing through the area one day, bought the site. He said he would build a fine summer house commanding a view of the great river flowing down from the green mountains. He sent for the best woodsmen in his logging concession near the headwaters of the river and told them to fell the trees.

The woodsmen took one look at those large trees and shook their heads. They said they would cut down any tree in the deepest woods but not those.

So Don Antonio sent for several of the best woodsmen in his Mindoro logging concession. He said he would pay them double their wages if they cleared the site for his summer mansion.

The men stood at the foot of the demon tree, hesitated, and finally said:

> *Bari-bari! Umarayyu kamu ngamin, afu.*
> *Arammi nga liwa ngem liwa ni Ama Tonio.*
> (Keep off, keep off, sirs, please.
> It's Old Man Tonio's wish that we fell these.)

All the trees were down by nightfall, for the men worked fast with machine saws. They lopped off the enormous branches and then had them laid side by side. They collected their wages and left town at once. Lumber and iron bars and cement arrived in trucks and the masons and carpenters started work on the mansion.

The workers camped on the site but their sleep was broken each night. Was it a stallion they heard galloping around their shed the night before? Did they hear the snorting of a ferocious boar? Did not a big, smelly goat stray into the area? And a horse they saw was headless—or was it a carabao or a goat?

Those who saw the stallion said it disappeared and then a tall, headless dark man stood in its place. The man grew toward the ground and then toward the sky. Soon it vanished, only to be replaced by a large dog with blue flame leaping out of its throat. In turn the dog became a fierce boar with thick bristles on its back and its eyes afire.

The rich man scornfully laughed off these wild tales each time he dropped in to see how the work was getting along. But he soon found that he had to double his workers' pay, for they threatened to leave before completing the job. In time the men sought the help of an old woman who, it was said, dealt with creatures of the other world. The woman poured a mixture of vinegar and crushed ginger, onion, garlic, pepper, and salt over the perimeter of the site, muttering secret words as she did so. With that the mysterious creature stopped coming. The house took shape and the rich man brought in his family from the big city to spend the summer and enjoy the magnificent view of the river from the verandah.

But it was said that the rich man had to have a new caretaker each year after his family moved back to the city. For the demon kept on coming back to its old haunts. Now it lived in one room, now in another, so that you never could tell where you might glimpse it by night.

The Pretender

INTO THE VILLAGE store stumbled Enteng and fainted. Those who sat swapping tales on the bamboo bench in front of the store fanned him with their palm-leaf hats and wiped his forehead with damp cloth. They washed off the mud on his feet and put medicine on his bruises.

At last he came to and told them that he had been tricked by a tikbalang. He said he had worked in his clearing on the slope of Mt. Makiling later than usual and his brother Daniel had come for him. Daniel said they must proceed to their Aunt Sianang's village because she was dead. "We have to go and join the vigil," Daniel had said.

Uphill and down dale they walked, but they did not seem to get any closer to their aunt's village. They passed by a tall kalumpang tree and Enteng recalled that they had passed the tree earlier that evening. "We aren't getting anywhere much," he said. "Oh, yes we are," replied the other. "We will be there after a couple of turns in the trail."

They walked some more. By and by Enteng saw a papaya tree that they had passed earlier. "I'm sure we have gone past this tree before," he said, sitting down to catch his breath.

Daniel sat down, too, and put his arm on Enteng's shoulder. Enteng touched the man's elbow and suddenly looked at him in terror, for that elbow was rough and hard. Only then did Enteng see that the man who said he was Daniel had too much hair on his nape to be a man.

Sweat suddenly broke out on Enteng's forehead and streamed down his back. He held the bottom of his shirt, bent over, and eased himself out of the shirt through its neck and armholes. But the night on the mountain was cold and so Enteng put on his shirt again, but he wore it inside out so that its dry surface would be next to his skin.

The man who had said he was Daniel looked at Enteng's reversed shirt and stood up. He told Enteng to wait and disappeared in the bushes beside the trail. Enteng felt too tired to walk on, so he leaned against a tree and rested.

The stranger never came back, and then Enteng knew it was a tikbalang which had pretended to be someone he knew and tried to lead him astray.

"What I cannot understand — is why the tikbalang left me," said Enteng.

An old man cleared his throat and replied: "It might have been because he thought you were another man and not the one he had been molesting after you put on your shirt inside out."

The Widow and the Tree Trunks

THE WIDOW MAYYANG lived alone in a little grass hut near a coconut grove. Her children had grown up, married, and gone off to live in homes they had built themselves. There was but a patch of roof over her head, and her kitchen had but one wall to keep the wind from blowing out the fire in her stove.

Tending the fire one dark evening, she became vaguely conscious of a pair of tree trunks standing next to her cooking shed. She wondered why they were there, having never been there before. Her eyesight had grown worse than ever, she thought. She touched the trunks, stretching her arms wide to reach them both. They were rough and hairy like trees covered with moss. But they quivered at her touch, and when she looked up she found that they were not trees but the legs of a huge pugot. The demon's dark body was etched against the sky and his green eyes glared down at her from among the stars, or so it seemed to her.

She closed her eyes and ran screaming. Her neighbors came to her aid with bamboo torches, but no trace of the demon remained except a heavy goat smell in the air.

Her sons made new walls for her kitchen and planted yellow ginger roots and red pepper shrubs under the eaves, and never again did the pugot ever come to molest her.

The Kapre Who Could Pray

A MAN WAS STRIDING HOME on a lonely country road
one night. A new moon glimmered beyond the trees
and he shivered, for a light shower was falling.

"They say one should not be about on a night like
this," he thought. "They say demons go about when a
moon shaped like a slice of watermelon is in the west
and a shower is falling."

By and by he sensed the fall of heavy footsteps. He
turned around and saw a large kapre loping after him.
Its large green eyes glowed in the night.

He quickened his steps, and the demon quickened
its steps, too.

He struck a match, two matches, and hopefully
looked back. The kapre was still there padding after
him.

He said snatches from a Latin prayer that, to be
frank about it, he had never succeeded in memorizing.
Still the kapre remained at his heels.

He pulled a prayer book out of his hip pocket,
opened the book, and intoned the Lord's Prayer. He
did not need to look back for he felt the kapre
breathing on the back of his neck.

Soon he was fairly yelling out the prayer from his book, but the kapre stepped to his side and said, "I can do better. I can recite that prayer from memory." Then it rattled off the prayer with its green eyes closed.

The man knew of nothing else to do. He dropped everything he had and ran.

Dragons

The Moon Eater

IN A CAVE deep in the mountains of the western Visayas there once lived an enormous snakelike dragon called the *bakunawa*. The cave opened to the dark forest on one side and to the blue sea on the other.

No one knew how old the dragon was, but the village folk often talked in awed whispers about its great size and length. Some hunters had glimpsed it asleep, its head and part of its upper coils showing among the trees, most of its huge body inside the cave, and its long tail swishing back and forth on the waters below.

Eight men went to the forest to gather rattan one day. Their folks waited for them till late at night and they waited all the next two days, but they did not return.

On the fourth day, three of the men came limping home. They were quaking with fear and their bodies were covered with bruises. They said they had seen the head of the enormous snake half hidden in its upper coils.

They had stood four on each side and shot their arrows into the half-closed eyes of the monster. The men on one side had succeeded in blinding the dragon in the left eye, but the men on the other side had missed their mark. Then the angry dragon had swiftly uncoiled and attacked the men on the side of its remaining good eye before they could hide.

"We escaped," said the men who managed to come home, "because we had time to hide in a hole which the bakunawa could not push its head into."

A monstrous hissing sound like the surge of a typhoon came echoing down the valley a few nights later, and the people knew that the bakunawa was rolling down to their village. They picked up their things and fled.

But just then, the full moon rose from the mountains. The dragon saw the big moon and stopped. It reared its huge body and rose above the trees. Higher and higher the dragon's body rose till it reached the moon above the clouds. Then the monster opened its wide mouth and snatched the moon. The moon grew red and the people were happy that the bakunawa did not proceed to their village.

But then they were struck with terror. "The bakunawa has bitten the moon!" they shouted. "The moon will bleed to death! Then we will have no moon at all. A world without a moon would be very ugly."

In a moment the bakunawa found the moon too hard to bite. So it spewed the moon out of its mouth. Then it came in huge coils down to earth and crawled back into its cave.

The people saw the moon grow bright like silver again. They stood up and danced and sang. "The bakunawa has left and we still have our moon!" they shouted with joy.

But not long after, on a dark night, the bakunawa silently crawled down to the village and devoured those who could not hide fast enough. Then the moon rose, and the dragon reached up for it and swallowed it, too, still thinking to eat it at last. But the moon was too hard to eat and the bakunawa crawled back into its cave.

This has gone on and on since then, and that, say the village folk, is why we have eclipses. When there is an eclipse of the moon, children leave their play and run home in great fear. When there is an eclipse of the sun, the pigs and goats run home in terror, the chickens fly into their tree roosts and crow as if it were evening, and the dogs, unable to understand what it is all about, howl out loud as if to ask why the night has come so soon.

And so the folk still hope that some brave hunter will blind the bakunawa in the other eye. Then it cannot see at all and will die.

The Sea-Eagle God

LONG, LONG AGO there were only the blue sky above and the dark ocean below. The sky smiled down at the ocean and the ocean smiled up at the sky. The two were very good friends for thousands of years.

One day a gray sea eagle, the great god Manaul, appeared in the wide space between the sky and the ocean. For many thousands of years the eagle god flew back and forth, back and forth between the sky and the ocean. Manaul flew without rest, for he could find nothing to rest on.

Then one day the friendship between the sky and the ocean ended, no one knows why. One morning the ocean tossed salty waves at the face of the sky. This made the sky angry, and it dropped heavy gray clouds on the face of the ocean. The sky and the ocean fought in this way for many thousands of years.

Every time the ocean rose to hit the sky, the great eagle god Manaul swooped down to the shallower water and picked up large rocks with his powerful talons. He dropped the rocks in different spots in the ocean.

At last the sky and the ocean got tired of fighting. The sky stopped dropping gray clouds on the ocean, and the ocean stopped tossing salt water up at the sky. For the first time after many thousands of years,

Manaul could rest on the piles of rock he had made in the ocean.

In time the piles of rock became land. Grass, shrubs, and trees grew upon the land, and now Manaul had cool places in which to rest when the day was warm.

One day a piece of green bamboo came drifting from across the wide ocean. The waves of the ocean tossed it back and forth and then cast it ashore on one of the islands that had been made. Before long a green shoot grew out of a knot in the bamboo. The shoot sent down its roots into the sand and slowly rose toward the sky. Its thin leaves cast a gray-green shadow on the sand, and the shoot became the first bamboo plant in the whole wide world. Manaul sat in the cool shade of the bamboo when the sun blazed overhead at noon.

Before long ago two adjoining bamboo joints began to swell. They grew larger and larger each day. Manaul patiently watched them swell and waited.

Then while Manaul sat resting in the cool shade, he
heard a knocking from inside the swollen bamboo. The
sound grew louder and louder. At last Manaul pecked
the joint with his strong, hooked beak. The joint split
open, and out stepped a man. The man stood brown,
erect, and large-muscled, and Manaul called him
Malakas, the Strong One. Malakas was the first man in
the world.

From the next lower joint Manaul heard soft
knocking sounds, too. He pecked at the joint, and it
split open and out stepped a beautiful woman. Her
skin was light brown, and she stood smiling sweetly on
the sand. Manaul called her Maganda, the Beautiful
One. Maganda was the first woman in the world.

The Visayans of old said that Malakas and Maganda
were the first parents of mankind and that Manaul was
the greatest god in the world.

Born of Two Breezes

IN THE BEGINNING the world was ruled by two gods, Kaptan and Maguayan. Fish swam in the sea and birds flew in the air. Soft breezes blew between the earth and the sky and made the world fresh and cool.

The land breeze and the sea breeze became one, and the land breeze gave birth to a slender reed floating in the water. The god Kaptan saw the reed, picked it up, and planted it in the ground. The reed grew and then broke into two. One piece became Lalaki, the first man, and the other became Babayi, the first woman.

Lalaki told Babayi one day, "Let us raise a family."

"We cannot raise a family," Babayi replied. "We came from the same reed. We are brother and sister."

"We are the only people in the world," said Lalaki. "The great god must have put us here to raise the first family in the world."

"Let's first ask the god of the sea and the god of the air, and then let us ask the great god at the foot of the tree that holds up the world."

"Yes, let us do so," Lalaki said. They walked to the sea and watched, and soon a god in the shape of a great big tuna came swimming by.

"Do you think we two can marry?" they asked the tuna god.

"Yes, you can," the tuna god said.

Lalaki and Babayi walked on and saw, sitting on a tree, a god in the shape of a dove.

"Do you think we two can marry?" they asked the god shaped like a dove. "We want to raise a family."

"Oh, yes, you can," said the dove god.

They thanked the dove god and walked down to the bottom of the world. Down, down, and down they walked until they saw a god in the shape of a huge python coiled around an enormous post. This post held up the whole world so that it would not sink to the bottom of the ocean. When the people in the world above did something wrong, the python god grew angry and shook the post, causing an earthquake in the world above.

Babayi was afraid of the snake god, but Lalaki told her it would do her no harm. "Look at its handsome coat," he said. "It looks like a beautiful sleeping mat."

The python saw them and asked, "What brings you two here?"

"We have a question to ask," said Lalaki.

"Ask it."

"Can she and I marry?" asked Lalaki, pointing to Babayi.

"Yes, you can," replied the snake god.

Lalaki and Babayi thanked the snake god and walked home. They got married, and their children and other descendants peopled the earth.

The Hunter and the Python

LONG AGO a Bontok youth entered his ancestors' woods to chop down a tree. He climbed up a slope and came to a stand of tall, straight trees. Unable to decide which tree he should cut down, he leaned his axe against a large tree and sat down on a moss-grown log for a more leisurely look. The log lay under big trees and was partly concealed by thick shrubs and vines.

By and by the log moved. "An earthquake," he
thought, but he wondered why the branches overhead
did not stir.

Then all at once the log he sat on reared its farther
end and swung around. In a moment its knobbed end
opened and became the huge mouth of an enormous
python.

He was inside the monster's mouth in a moment
and was inexorably sliding down its gullet. He was so
small in comparison that he quickly got into the
python's stomach.

He knew he must do something fast or suffocate.
Taking his hip knife, he slashed into the wall of the
creature's crop and skin and squirmed through.

The man thought the python would be waiting to
snatch him back and swallow him again as he came
out. But to his surprise, he saw the monster coiled in a
heap like an enormous rope, sound asleep. It evidently
did not mind its wound.

He looked around and found his sharp headaxe
leaning against the tree where he had left it. He ran for
it and then, carefully aiming at the base of the python's
spear of a head, swung the shiny axe. He severed the
monster's head with three swift smashes.

Then the creature's body uncoiled, thrashed blindly
about, and writhed and whirled, seeking him out. But
he stood at a safe distance, calmly whittling away the
spikes of a rattan twine.

At last the python became still. He walked to the
severed head, threaded it through one huge eye and out
of the cavernous mouth, and then dragged it down to
his village.

The people saw the monstrous head and danced
with joy. They knew that the fearful creature that had
depleted their numbers and devastated their livestock
was dead.

The young man married the fairest daughter of the
village chief and in due time became chief after him.

Dwarfs

The Tuba Thief

A MAN ENTERED a coconut grove to gather palm wine one evening. He paused under a tree for a few puffs on his rolled cigar.

Then he crushed the glowing head of his cigar against the tree, tucked what remained of the cigar in the lining of his hat, and climbed up the tree.

But when he looked into the node, he found it empty. "Someone has been poaching here," he muttered.

It was the same way the next evening and the evening after, and the tuba gatherer vowed to catch the thief. He walked to the grove before sunset and lay down on his belly under a thick bush.

By and by a bearded little man, not much over two feet tall, a plump and wrinkle-faced fellow too old for his child's height, came. The stranger climbed the tree containing the node the tuba oozed into and pulled out the trimmed panicle from which the sweetish red liquor had dripped during the day. Then he raised the node, tossed back his sparsely bearded head, and made a long swig.

He emptied the node at one take and hung it from the panicle again, tucking in its cut ends, and scrambled down from the tree.

Quietly unsheathing his bolo, the man leaped out of
the bush and ran after the thief. But it fled with the
greatest of ease, disappeared behind a large *pitogo* tree
and was gone.

When the man got home and told his master that
the tuba node was empty and he had seen the thief, the
master smiled knowingly, nodded his head and said,
"Go slow on that palm sap. Some have fallen from the
trees and broken their necks for drinking it up there."

The Dwarf Who Wanted Meat

ONE MORNING a barefoot maiden of fifteen walked to the town market to buy some fish and meat. Her return home was delayed somewhat because the fisherfolk were slow in coming back from the sea. The shadows had each gathered to its own tree when she hurried back to her village.

She left the hot trail to walk where there were patches of grass so she would not burn her soles. At the foot of a big rock, she suddenly came face to face with a knee-tall wrinkled old man with a long white beard. The little old man held out a handful of gold and said, "Take pure gold for a portion of meat, pretty maid."

The girl blinked in disbelief but when she opened her eyes the dwarf still stood there offering her his handful of gold. Then she knew that it was true and became frightened. She turned and tried to run but her legs would not move.

"I said take a handful of pure gold for a little meat, pretty maid," the dwarf repeated.

She had heard that a girl who gave anything to a dwarf would be lost to dwarfland forever. But dwarfs were said to fear saltwater fish and she replied, "I haven't got any meat here, sir. But I have some fresh

fish from the sea. I will be glad to let you have some
and you can keep your gold."

The dwarf shook his head testily. "I want no fish,"
he said. Then he pointed at the basket and added, "All
I want is some meat, and I know you have some in
there."

Again the girl turned and tried to run, but she could
not lift her feet. Then she stooped as if to put down
her basket, but she quickly scooped up some dirt with
her hand and cast it into the dwarf's big eyes.

When the dust cleared, the dwarf was nowhere to
be seen, but the girl, frightened out of her wits, had
slumped to the ground in a dead faint.

A man came driving down in his cart and found her
there. He gathered her up and made the dust of the
road fly with his carabao's hoofs. The girl came to in
due time, but she had a blank stare and could not
speak.

The folk said her spirit had been stolen by the old
man of the rocks and she never got well again.

The Angry Dwarf

A YELLOW GUAVA as big as a girl's fist had smiled from across the fence all day long. But the cross old man who owned the tree was constantly at his window and did not give the little girl a chance to climb over the fence and get it.

After the chickens had flown into their roosts and the old man shut his window, she slipped over the fence and tiptoed to the tree as quietly as the dry leaves would let her.

But the fruit was higher than it had looked from her window and so she stepped on a termite mound to reach for the fruit. Then a tiny high-pitched voice said: "*Aray! Aray!*" and she felt a sharp pinch on her ankle. She looked down and there stood a little old man with a long, sparse beard glaring at her with his fiery big eyes.

The girl ran home and told her mother, who next day baked a *bibingka* into which she put no salt and sugar but a double helping of grated coconut meat. After sunset she asked her tart old neighbor to let her daughter place the bibingka on the mound under his guava tree.

"Please forgive me, sir," said the girl to no one, putting the rice cake on top of the mound. "I didn't know you lived here. I stepped on the mound not to annoy you but to reach for the ripe guava on the tree."

"It's all right with me," she heard the high-pitched voice of an old man say. "But from now on, never get what isn't yours. And be sure you beg pardon when you walk through places where people seldom go."

The Disappearing Maid

ASYANG, a maid with dimpled cheeks when she smiled
and a tinkling voice when she laughed, walked to
dump kitchen trash at the end of the village street. She
was gone a long time and came back panting for breath.
Her feet were muddy and grass seeds had stitched
themselves into the hem of her skirt.

The next day she held a red clay jar against her hip
with an elbow and walked to the river for drinking
water out of the shallow well there. Again she came
home long after sunset and, when asked why, said she
had lost her way and walked through plowed fields
and open pastures, the jar of water perched on top of
her head.

Her mistress told her to stay indoors. She did so,
but after nightfall she slipped down the ladder with a
bowl of stewed fish and a plate of soft rice and tiptoed
out of the gate. There were wild meadow flowers in
her topknot when she came home.

Then her mistress kept an eye on her. For a week
she remained in the house, cooking, sweeping the floor,
washing the dishes, and mending clothes. The mistress
herself threw the trash away, washed the clothes, and
fetched drinking water from the river well. But a few
afternoons later, Asyang was caught slipping out into
the fields again. When asked where she was going, she
replied haughtily:

"To my lover's home in the bright city under the earth where my lover stands waiting to marry me."

"What lover are you talking about, stupid?" her mistress asked.

"He may not be handsome," Asyang replied, "and he may be short and his hands may be coarsed from mining for gold and precious stones in the earth, and his teeth may be few and weak and cannot grind anything but soft rice. But he is rich and loves me and that is all I care about." There was an unearthly twinkle in her eyes as she shouted her defiance.

Then she ran away. The men found her capering beside an anthill under an old tree in the middle of a field. They held her firmly and took her home.

But Asyang was never herself again.

The Ardent Wooer

TESSIE, gay as a songbird in the reaping time, met her first suitor in Leyte on April 5, 1966, a day she was never to forget because her life took a dramatic turn then. She was sweeping the yard at the wink of day when she saw a bearded old man, eyes atwinkle and not quite level with her knees.

She had started to run away when she heard him say in a tenor voice, "Don't you run, Tessie. I intend no harm."

She wondered that the stranger should know her name, and he seemed to read her thoughts, for he added:

"I have often heard people call you by that sweet name. Be not afraid, for I am a friend."

Tessie was moved by his courtesy. She felt funny to be standing so tall over a man. But she surveyed his features—skin a dark brown, ears shaped like those of a mouse, eyes puffed like mushroom buttons just out of the turf, nose flaring, and toes far apart. Tessie turned to go, but the fellow pleaded: "Let's be friends, Tessie. That's all I ask."

She hesitated, opened her mouth to say no, and ended by nodding. Well she knew that if she refused his friendship he could make her throb with fevers and chills, roll on the floor with itches, or lie in bed the rest of her life all but dead in a paralytic stroke. "Can I go?" she said.

"You can," he replied. "But let's meet again soon."

A week went by without further incident. Then one day when she was out chasing grasshoppers beyond the fence, there she saw him flashing his toothy smile at her from under a shrub. This time he wore a basket hat tipped with a shiny stud of gold, and his clothes shimmered with gems. "I'm an old hand at mistress-winning and I waste no words," he began without ceremony. "I love you and want you to be my bride. I know I'm not much to look at, but there is plenty of treasure in my home for you." He tried to reach up for her hand but she screamed, ran, and flew up the stairs.

A week later she was embroidering on a circular frame at the bottom of the kitchen ladder when she heard his tenor voice. He was singing a love song under a *kamia* herb. "Come, Tessie," he sang, his knobby arms pompously extended toward her. "Come to me!"

"Leave me alone, old man!" she shouted impulsively. "Leave me!"

He did, and Tessie expected that she would quickly become ill for her rudeness, but she did not. Each night after everybody else was asleep, however, he sat at her bedside whispering, "Come away with me, Tessie! Come away with me."

The shine left Tessie's eyes and her laughter was gone. Constantly ill at ease, she jerked whenever she heard the slightest rustle of leaves.

The priest came chanting Latin verses to exorcise evil spirits he did not name. He sprinkled holy water and tossed a censer around the house and in the yard.

For a month Tessie's persistent suitor did not show up and her face started to regain its glow. But one day while she sat in her room, a pebble fell at her feet. It was bluish green and jewel-like, such as she had often seen in the brook just outside the town when she and her friends went swimming there.

She started shaking with terror, knowing too well
that her ardent wooer was back. There was a fresh
fragrance in the air when she got out of bed next
morning.

The folk healer was sent for then, and he said that
her suitor was about to redouble his courtship. Tessie's
parents quietly packed up her things and took her on
the long boatride to Manila. There they found her a job
in an office where, said the healer, her suitor could not
get in because of the crowds.

For some days it happened as the healer had said.
But soon Tessie's suitor got there too and continued his
relentless wooing. The other employees grew disturbed
about this pretty provincial girl who had an odd habit
of talking to herself at work.

The company doctor had some quiet sessions with
her and sent for her parents. He told them Tessie
should not be working in an office where the schedule
was tight and the job might be monotonous. "She
should get some rest in a quiet institution," he added.

And so to an institution she next went. It was some
distance from the noisy city. A stone wall lined with
green shrubbery surrounded the site where specialists
attended to her. In due time it was noted with great
satisfaction that though her suitor still called on her, his
visits became less and less frequent. She was well
enough to go home before Christmas.

She is married to a town youth now and has a
daughter who promises to be as pretty and tall as she.
Never again has her truncated elderly wooer molested
her.

The Dwarf Who Liked Bibingka

AN OLD WOMAN made bibingka for people who passed by her gate on their way to their fields early each morning. Before going to bed she ground the soaked rice in a two-piece stone hard mill. She poured some of the rice into a hole in the upper piece, turned the handle slowly while pouring in a little water now and then to keep the grinders wet, and let the ground rice ooze thickly into a clay bowl. When she had done, she mixed in some rice yeast and let the mixture stand overnight.

She woke up before cockcrow and grated a coconut on a grating horse. Into a bowl she squeezed out the milk from a few handfuls of coconut meat for greasing the bibingka when it turned a nice brown and was almost ready. Then she threw the dry meat out of the window for the chickens to pick up in the morning.

After that she mixed the rest of the coconut meat with the ground rice. She then sprinkled a handful of sugar into the mix, stirred it, and she was ready to go out and bake her bibingka. Using charcoal from coconut shells and wood, she built a fire on a tin plate. She built another fire in a stove formed by three stones. She put a clay pan over the stove and on the pan the burning tin plate. When the pan was properly heated, she took down the burning plate. She spread a circular

piece of banana leaf on the pan and poured in enough
cake mix to make a good bibingka.

One early morning when she threw the dry coconut
meat out of the window, she forgot to say "Keep off!
Keep off!" It happened that a little old man had come
out of the termite mound under the bamboo tree behind
the house and was standing under the eaves. He had a
long thin beard, a big nose, and large hands and feet.

At noon and after sundown, dwarfs, it is said, often enter people's yards to listen to what is being said indoors. When they hear folks say nice things about little girls who have nice names and sweet voices, besides, they know which girls they should entice into their dwarf realm.

The dwarf whom the old woman hit with the coconut meat squeezed dry waited for her. When she came out he walked to her and demanded, "Why did you throw out the coconut meat without warning me?"

She said she was very sorry. "Were you badly hurt, sir?" she asked with great anxiety, for she had heard that dwarfs return whatever injury they receive in exactly equal amount.

"Badly, badly!" he said. "Some of the coconut got into my eyes, and my eyes are not much as they are." Then he added severely: "Nice people should not throw things out of their windows. We dwarf folk never do."

"It will never happen again," she replied. "What can I do to show how sorry I am?"

The old fellow's reply was prompt. "I just want a little piece of your bibingka each morning," he said. "Put no spices in it and just leave it on the mound in your backyard while it is still hot."

"I'll gladly do that," the old woman replied.

He walked to the backyard and was gone.

After that the old woman was careful to put a piece of hot bibingka on the mound each morning. She was careful, when she swept the yard or walked about at noon or after dark to say "Keep off! Keep off!"

And she never threw rubbish out of her windows again.

A Day in Dwarf Town

A LITTLE GIRL was playing *piko* near a termite mound in the backyard. It was midday and she should have been taking a nap instead of playing near the mound and annoying the old men who lived underground and often came out through a hole in the mound.

She tossed her piko stone too far out and hit the mound. As she bent down to pick it up, an old man three spans tall came from behind the mound and stood before her. He had brown pants on, a red coat embroidered with gold threads, and a helmet of white gourd shell tipped with a shiny gold stud.

She was at the point of running away when the little man said, "Don't you be afraid, pretty girl. Come and see dwarf town with me."

He led her into the mound through a tiny hole concealed by a dry leaf. Down, down, down they went through a maze of winding paths.

At last they came to a beautiful town with narrow streets paved with silver and gold and with rubies, sapphires, and emeralds. The houses on both sides of the street stood only up to her head, but they were made of gold and silver and precious stones.

They entered a house and little old men came to welcome her. They wore bright clothes lined with rich gold thread like the coat of the little man who had

brought her in. They ate at a table so low that they did
not have to sit on chairs. Their food was placed on
gold and silver plates, and their soup was in bowls of
precious metals, too.

They offered her food to eat, and she thanked them
but she shook her head politely, saying she had just had
her noon meal and was not hungry.

She did not feel at home in this strange town of
little old men with big hands and feet. Their large eyes
could not see well, but their big round ears heard the
faintest sounds. They had no spices in their food and it
smelled flat.

They brought handfuls of precious stones to her.
They put strings of jewels around her wrists, ankles,
and neck. But the place and the people looked so
strange that she soon started to weep.

"Don't weep, pretty girl," they said. "Make our
town your town. Live with us, and our wealth will all
be yours."

She politely dried her tears and smiled.

The next day the dwarfs said they were sorry she

was not happy in their town. The messenger would take her back to her village.

Before she left, they presented her with jewels in a red kerchief, its four corners bunched in a knot. "These are our parting gift to you," they said. "Keep them so you won't forget your friends in dwarf town. But tell no one that you have been here and that these are from us."

She thanked them all for being so kind and said goodbye. Then the messenger led her through the same winding path by which she had come.

Her parents found her asleep beside the mound next day. In one hand she gripped a bright red kerchief. They awakened her and she suddenly jumped and shouted: "A gift from dwarf town! A gift from dwarf town!"

They took her kerchief from her and untied the knot. It was charcoal they found and nothing else, but they were overjoyed to see their daughter again. They said they had spent an entire month looking for her, and then she knew that a day in dwarf town was a month in people town.

Marina's First Suitor

MARINA RODRIGUEZ, a Eurasian, was fourteen in 1960 when she met her first suitor. She was playing hide-and-seek with other girls beside her father's old warehouse one afternoon when a little man suddenly stood before her.

"Look at him!" she exclaimed. "Look at the funny little man!"

Her playmates came out of hiding and looked but saw no one. "Come now, close your eyes tight so we can hide," they told Marina.

But she did not mind them. She pointed at the pompous little stranger and kept on giggling.

The look on her playmates' faces darkened. "What's the matter, Marina?" they asked.

"But it's true—aha, ahee-hee-hee!" she added, for two more men stood before her, two little men not two feet tall, with greenish skin, long green beards, and blue eyes. They rather resembled the little men in the picture book her father had bought her on her visit to Spain some years before. The first dwarf was decked in the ornate attire of a king, and the other two wore the costume of foot soldiers in a *comedia*.

At last the three little men disappeared and Marina joined her playmates. But the picture of the three curious little fellows remained at the back of her mind.

The dwarf king visited her the following Sunday while she was in the bathroom. He made her promise not to tell anyone about his visit. "Something I should be very sorry for will happen to you if you tell," he warned her.

At first his visits came once a week and then each night. Her parents noticed that there was a darting quickness in Marina's glance and this disturbed them. They also saw that she was having difficulty recognizing people who spoke to her.

"He is Don Alfonso," she finally admitted to them, "king of the dwarfs. He promised to give me riches and power if I agreed to be his queen."

They took her to a Manila psychiatrist. The young doctor questioned her at some length and then advised her parents to be gentle to her and keep her under observation. "She will probably pull out of it in time," he assured them. "It's part of her growing up."

At his suggestion they got Marina a nurse to sleep in her room with her, and this angered her dwarf lover. He would slip into the room, creep into the nurse's bed, and pinch her until she shrieked in hysterics.

So Marina's parents put her under the care of an aunt living on the other side of town. This arrangement seemed to work, but only for a few days. One afternoon while she sat reading a story book in the sala her royal suitor suddenly appeared and sat in the divan in front of her.

"How did you trace my whereabouts?" she asked him.

"A king has ways of finding out," he replied, his beady blue eyes atwinkle.

Marina saw him stroke his long beard and she grew curious. "By the way, what makes you keep such a bushy beard?" she asked. "Doesn't it get into your soup?"

"My beard is the source of my power," he replied. "Royalty eats without getting messed up with his beard."

"That reminds me. You once said you would give
me power if I became your queen. What did you mean
by that?"

"I will give you all the power you ask for if you
marry me. I will make you invisible when you wish
and pass through keyholes and crevices in the ground.
I will give you all the gold you want—and gold is
power—and the power to sing like a diva and dance
like a ballet queen."

Then the dwarf made her sing and dance, and she
sang with such fire and danced with such flurry that
the neighbors came running. One and all they said
they had never thought such singing and dancing pos-
sible.

Marina's folks became more worried than ever, and
as a last recourse they sent for the herb healer who
claimed commerce with the dark gods of the ancient
earth. He came to look her over and left without a
word. He returned early next day, made them vow to
tell no one what he was about to let them know, and
then whispered: "The dwarf king said he wants to
marry your daughter."

"But she is just fourteen!" her father remonstrated,
ill able to conceal his shock.

"Fourteen is not too early," replied the healer. "My
grandmother was twelve when she married my
grandfather." Then he whispered a few more words in
Marina's father's ear, and as a result the boys in the
neighborhood, youths with swarthy faces and dark hair
but big and muscular, were allowed to call on her in
the evenings. The house was stoned a number of times
while her human callers were up there with her. The
healer assured them that their dwarf rival was trying to
frighten them off and they should not mind him.

Before long only the handsomest and tallest of the
boys remained and at last the dwarf stopped coming.
Then her spells of absentmindedness came farther apart,
in a year she married the man, and at the wedding
everybody sighed with relief because the dwarf did not
molest her again.

But her first baby came and the dwarf king started
to make trouble anew. The healer said the little old
man wanted Marina's child to assuage his hurt. "But
we can give him something to pacify him," said he.
"Make some rice cakes fit for an old man. Put no
seasoning in it so that his digestion will not be ruined
and you will not be suspect of trying to poison him.
Put the food in a wicker and place it in the old
warehouse."

This was done, and the dwarf never came again.

Elves

The Elf Maiden

A YOUTH was harvesting rice all by himself in his field on the thither side of the river one late afternoon when he heard the tinkle of a tiny bell beside him. He stopped and looked but saw no one.

He returned to his work wondering whether the sound of the bell was only in his head, but after a while he heard it again. He looked under the rice plants and behind the dike but saw no one there.

Before long the thin fragrance of cooking reached him. Then he looked again and saw a pretty girl standing right behind him. She had wavy, copper-colored hair, a light skin, and a dainty face. She held out a basket of food to him and said:

"My father sends you this gift with his greetings."

The youth stared at her dumbfounded and finally said, "I am sorry but I can't take food from a stranger."

"I am not a stranger," she replied. "I am the daughter of your neighbor the king. He asks you to come with me."

Then the youth knew she was an elf-maiden, and he was frightened. He took his burden basket, swung it over his shoulder, and ran. His heart beat so fast that he fainted on the way and fell.

There his neighbors, walking home from their fields at dewfall, found him and carried him home.

He lay abed many days and nights. He told them
that the elf-maiden sat by his bed day and night and
kept on asking him to let her show him the way to her
father's happy realm.

The young man's relatives sent for an old man who
knew the secrets of the creatures of midnight. The old
man touched the youth's forehead and said:

"An elf-princess has indeed fallen in love with this
young man. Take him to a village on the other side of
the mountains or he will never be rid of her."

His folk put him on a carabao cart and hurried him
off to his uncle's on the other side of the mountains.
On the youth's farm the old man killed a white hen and
boiled its meat together with soft-grained rice. He put
not a pinch of salt or pepper and not a chip of ginger
to season the dish with. Then he bore the food to a
grove hard by the young man's old farm at sundown,
whispering secret words to the invisible folk who lived
there.

The youth was soon back on his feet and in due
time found a girl and married her. Never again did he
set foot on his native village for fear of the elf-king's
daughter whom he had spurned.

The Elf Voyagers

KADIO HAD LINGERED in town a little too long that Saturday evening and had drunk perhaps too many cups of cane wine. But now he and his dog were on the footpath leading back to the village up on a mountain slope.

It was well past midnight when man and dog reached a large mango tree about which many a legend had been whispered by the village folk. But Kadio told himself that he was not one given to believing old tales about creatures of midnight and walked on.

Near the tree the dog stopped short, raised its muzzle, and sent up a mournful howl. Kadio recalled a legend about

what a dog saw when it howled like that. If you were
brave and wanted to see what the dog was howling at,
said the old folk, you should rub the eyes of the dog
with your forefinger, then rub your eyes with the same
finger, and look from between your legs.

Unbelieving but curious, Kadio held his dog firmly
between his legs and did so. Then he let the dog go
and looked up at the mango tree between his legs as he
bent down.

There, with bright sails spread out in the clear
moonlight, stood a tall ship. It sailed through the air
and headed for the top of the tree. It floated as if the
air were a transparent sea.

In a few moments the boat lowered its sails. A
crewman with a gay uniform leaped to the tree and tied
the boat to the top branch. Then one by one the air
voyagers, good-looking men and women who sailed
through the air by night, stepped lightly from the boat
to the tree. They sang and danced while they des-
cended to the foot of the tree as if the tree were a
staircase lighted by fireflies. They politely took their
turn, and before long every passenger had disembarked
and danced his way into the shadows.

Then from the shadows other elves in pretty clothes
appeared. They danced up the tree and skipped aboard
the ship.

When everyone had gone on board, the crewman
untied the boat and it sailed gracefully away in the sky.

Kadio's dog stopped howling then, and Kadio led it
to his village wondering where those elves had gone.

The Elf Lover

AN OLD FARMER was dying and called for his three
daughters. "I give you my farm," he said. "But never
leave it, for I had a hard time clearing the trees from it."

Nine days after the burial, the youngest daughter,
the prettiest of the three, told her sisters that a good-
looking youth had proposed to her the evening before.
She said he was tall, his nose high, and his skin so
white and delicate you could see the water trickling
down his throat as he drank.

Her sisters glanced at each other uneasily. "You
had better stay in bed," they told her.

A few days later, she said her suitor's folks had
come to ask her to marry their son. She wanted to
know what her sisters thought she should do, for they
were to return for her answer that night.

"Tell them you can't marry him," they said. They
were certain these folk only existed in her mind.

That night the girl said that sweet, soft music was
playing under her window. She peeped coyly out and
said she saw gorgeously dressed people in the yard.
Her sisters looked out of the window but saw only
darkness there.

Next morning they found their poor sister dead in
the fields. There were no bruises on her body, and the
neighbors said her elf-lover had come and taken her
soul away.

The Encantada

A TAXI DRIVER sat slapping his ears and arms at the bus station. The mosquitoes were increasing every minute and it must be getting late. He wondered what the college girls would be wearing this summer when they came home for vacation.

At last the bus from Aklan pulled in and quickly emptied itself. Four girls, all pretty and taller than most, carried their suitcases to his taxi. He put their luggage in the trunk and they got in. Then he got in too and turned to the girl on the front seat beside him to ask where and to admire her delicate profile at a glance.

"Dilum," she said, a dimple flickering on her cheek.

Dilum was a village five kilometers from town. He wondered if he heard right and repeated his questioning glance.

"That's right—Dilum," those at the back chorused.

He knew just where Dilum was, of course—a sleepy cluster of nipa huts at the far end of a dirt road and cuddling right next to the woods. It was, to be sure, just the place for a quiet summer vacation far from the jostle of towns. These city girls had perhaps been met by their provincial friend at the station but the friend perhaps left when the bus failed to get in on time. Were they going to be long in Dilum, he was going to

ask, but just then they started an animated conversation in Spanish and he listened to the merry tinkle of their voices.

They were from Manila, he gathered. It must be fun to drive a taxi where such pretty passengers abounded. Words came tumbling from their lips like musical notes into water, and wasn't their perfume exotic?

They stopped the taxi at the edge of an open field just before he turned into Dilum proper. He got out, opened the door for them, and handed out their luggage from the trunk. They paid the fare, adding a handsome tip. Then they took off from the gravel road straight into the open fields, so that he had to ask with some anxiety if they knew the way.

"Yes, we do!" they replied from the dark, their voices tinkling and fading into a whistled sweetness.

Thoughtfully he turned his taxi halfway round and beamed his lights to illuminate at least part of their way across the muddy fields.

His heart leaped to his throat, for they were gone.

The Bean Thief

A YOUNG FARMER left the fish he was stewing and hurried out to gather some tender pods from his bean rows. There was a slight fall of rain but the moon shone through from over the eastern hills.

He had passed this way in the afternoon and seen the first few pods, but now he saw none at all as he walked alongside the rows. "Someone has been picking them," he thought over a supper of boiled rice and stewed fish.

He had an early supper next day and hid in a bush at the farther end of his bean field. By and by the moon rose. A scent of wild flowers and a rustle of leaves came to him and then, out of the shadows, a slender woman in white stepped lightly toward the beans. She paused, looked this way and that with swift, birdlike movements, and started picking the beans.

With a leap and a bound he was out of the bush and at her side.

She stopped picking and said, "Oh, it's you." Her voice was soft and not a little like a whistled sound. She had a slender figure, her hair cascaded to her heels and on her arm hung a reed basket. She seemed entirely unafraid.

"I wondered who had been picking my beans," he said.

"I am sorry," she replied, "but I thought the beans just grew. Now I know they are yours and I want to ask some for my stew."

To make sure he was not dreaming, he asked, "Who are you and why do you come picking beans like a peasant's daughter?"

"You do not know then," she said with a little laugh. "You and I have often met on your way from the fields after sundown."

He was sure he had never seen her before. But since she said they had often met, he might have been just forgetful. So he said, "My eyes are a little weak."

"But now you remember and it's all right," she said. "To pay you for the beans, let me take you to my parents' home for a short visit," she added.

"And where do you live?" he asked.

"You will find out in a moment. Come, there's nothing to fear." She touched his arm and led him unresisting into a little grove near his vegetable patch.

She paused at the foot of a *bagbagutot* bush and took a quick step, and the bush was instantly a dimly lighted stairway. Now he knew she was the prettiest woman he had ever seen. Her skin was light brown, her hair wavy and long, quite brushing her heels with its tip, and her nose high and thin. Her teeth were a bright yellow gold.

There was soft, inviting music from the mansion overhead. Following her, he entered a hall. She led him past good-looking men and women who danced and talked and drank in their bright, old-fashioned costumes. Their brown hair was long like hers, and their skin was the color of copper. They were all quite as handsome as she. They were elves dwelling in mansions which were trees to mortal eyes.

Past an orchestra that played old music on odd-shaped instruments, she led him on till they finally came to a table laden with food yellow and red and black but with no fragrance.

She offered him rice and meat and he took some. But there was no salt or spices to them so that he ate just enough to be nice. Next she offered him a dessert of charcoal-black rice in a golden bowl. He shook his head at this, for the grains wriggled a little.

"Do take some," she insisted with a sweet smile.

But he shook his head again, and when he did so, the world spun and he fell to the floor.

His neighbors found him lying on his back under the bagbagutot bush next day. There was a wild shine in his eyes and he could not speak. It was weeks before his power of speech returned, and then he told them about his adventure in elf country.

The old folks smiled when he had done telling them his tale. Just as they thought, said they, an elf maiden, the *kaiba-an*, had taken a fancy to him and tried to seduce him. He would have been lost forever if he had eaten of the black rice she offered him.

The Maidens of the Fields

IN MASBATE a youth was walking under a tree at sunset when his breath caught, for not ten paces from him suddenly appeared three beautiful maidens. They looked like folk from a distant time and a far country. Such strange beauty and wild grace as theirs he had never before seen, and he stood in rapt admiration.

They walked to a brook and their dainty white feet and legs arched into the water. Then they hid briefly behind reeds, and when their heads and shoulders emerged again, they had taken off their clothes and hung them up on the reed panicles at the farther brim. With their cupped hands they dipped water over their shoulders like sparrows, talking together as they did so. Their maiden voices were soft as a shower on grass, and the man knew they were what the village folk called the maidens of the fields.

One of the maidens looked in his direction after a while and saw him. She turned to her companions and they briefly whispered among themselves. From their careful avoidance, he knew it was about him they talked.

After that they bathed some more in that sparrow-like manner of theirs. Then they reached up for their clothes and put these on. They leaned over the bank on their light feet and in a moment were capering straight toward him.

Just then his eyes smarted as if dirt had been cast into them. He fluttered his eyelids and wiped his eyes with the back of his hand, and the maidens had vanished when he looked again.

He walked to the brook, bent over it, and winked several times in the water. But that did not help any and he hurried home.

His wife smiled unbelieving when he told her whom he had seen, and she wondered what he had really been up to.

But she sent for Iya Minang, the herb healer, who promptly came and chewed a betel leaf with a pinch of lime and three cubes of areca nut. While she chewed these, she had the wife heat some drinking water over the wood stove. Then she poured the water into a coconut bowl, leaving in only the dregs, and had him bend over and flutter his eyelids in the liquid warmth.

At last she said, "That will do," held his head under her mouth, and breathed the sweet aroma of her betel chew into his open eyes. The sensation was soothing and he rose to find the dirt and the smarting in his eyes gone.

He thought that would be his only encounter with the maidens of the fields. But a few weeks later, while he stood under a tree surveying his maturing rice crop, they appeared again, danced toward the brook, hid behind the reeds for a quick moment, came out, and with their hands dipped water over their shoulders. They were even prettier in the noon light than they had been in the sunset light.

Then they put on their pretty dresses and swung gracefully up the bank and in their dancing gait were next moment heading straight toward him. Their dresses, of a distant age and a far place, rippled in the breeze. Their dark eyes had a bright glitter, and their teeth a strange but delightful sparkle.

But then as before his eyes smarted and he winked. They were gone when he looked again, and dirt seemed to fill his eyes.

Blindly he shuffled into the brook to wash the dirt out. But there was no help in that and his eyes hurt even worse.

His wife found him groping his way and led him home. She sent for Iya Minang, and the healer repeated her cure and got the dirt out of his eyes.

But as she turned to go, "Take care how you use your eyes, young man," said she. "You may not be so lucky next time."

The Rice Thieves

THE WARM DAYS were over at last and the season of long rains would soon be at hand. "It's time to fill the bin with clean white rice against the rainy days," the old wife told her husband. "Do bring out for me a *pungo* from the granary before you leave for the fields in the morning."

He was a quiet old man and made no reply, but at cockcrow before he set out for his plowing, he opened the granary and brought out a big bundle of rice beads.

While her pot of rice was cooking in the clay stove, she fed the pigs with bran and boiled *kangkong* and the chickens with grain. She swept the yard with a broom of bamboo twigs while her ginger tea was brewing. Then she roasted a dried fish over the red coals, and she had breakfast.

Soon the sun peeped over the mountains. She untied the pungo and separated the six fistfuls of smaller bundles—the *bettek*—it was made of. In the fenced-off strip of turf the chickens could not get into, she stood the bettek on end like big brown flowers. The rice heads in the heart of each bettek were crisp and dry by midmorning, and then she overturned the bettek to sun the outer heads, too.

In the afternoon after a wink of a nap she carried the bettek to a hollow log under the kitchen. She chose

a pestle and laid one bettek in the log. She held down
the bettek with one foot and pounded the grains loose,
unerringly hitting them rather than her big toe.

Soon all six bettek were threshed and she put the
grain in a basket. With cool, caressing long notes she
whistled for the wind. It came like a docile beast in
due time, and she winnowed out the chaff with the
wind's help. Then she pounded the grains in a wooden
mortar three coconut bowls of grain at a time. That
took a good part of the afternoon, for it was a tedious
task and she often had to pause for breath. When she
had done, she took the winnowing basket and sifted out
the bran for the fowls and pigs. Then she whistled for
the wind again and had it help her throw out the chaff
by tossing the pounded grain into the air with a
shallow basket.

The woman had a hard day, but she felt good when
she poured the hulled rice carefully into the bin and it
filled more than half of that. She put a chopping block
over the mouth of the bin and set about cooking
supper.

"Bring me down another pungo in the morning early," she asked her husband when he came home from the fields. "The bin will be filled before you get home tonight."

He brought down a second pungo. She dried the six smaller bundles of rice heads from it and then threshed, pounded, and cleaned them. But when, expecting to fill the bin, she poured the rice in, the rice got up to only the bin's shoulder.

She leveled the rice carefully with her hand and covered the bin's mouth with the chopping block.

"The pungo do not seem to be big enough this year," she told her husband in the evening. "Do bring down another pungo from the rice house early in the morning. The grain from it should certainly fill the bin and leave me some for my immediate cooking needs."

She dried, pounded, and cleaned the rice from the third pungo, but at sunset when she slid the rice into the bin, the bin was still unfilled.

"Someone has been stealing rice from this bin," she thought. She leveled the clean rice, placed a shiny brown bowl face down on it, and put the old chopping block over the mouth of the bin. But very early next day, as soon as her husband rose to pick up his things and set out for the fields, she lighted a torch of straw. She held the torch close to the foot of the ladder, and sure enough, on the soft earth were footprints. They were as tiny as those of babies. She followed the prints and saw that the lighter ones pointed to the bagbagutot bush, known to be the stairway of the elvish *ugaw* to the big *bulala* tree hard by the river. Over them lay heavier prints, and they pointed away from the bush.

The old woman tiptoed to her bin. The chopping block still covered its mouth, but the coconut bowl had been pushed to one side and there was less rice there than when she left the bin the evening before.

It was clear. The feet of the ugaw were known to be set wrong end forward. The light prints pointed away from the ladder and so the creatures must have

walked to the ladder empty-handed. Since the wee
folks' heavier footprints pointed to the ladder, they had
left the house laden with the rice they had stolen from
her bin.

She pounded a fourth bundle of rice the next day.
She poured the clean rice into the bin as before. She
placed the coconut bowl face down on top of the rice
and set the block over the bin's mouth. But meanwhile,
her husband had made a quick trip to the seaside.
There he filled his pockets with little white shells and
strung them on a twine. She hung the string of shells
around the neck of the bin and the shells made a jingle
when shaken. When the little folk came to steal rice
from her bin, they would brush against the shells by
accident, making the shells ring. The sound would
remind them of the salt from the sea, and of salt they
were in great dread.

No wee folk ever came to steal rice from the old
woman's bin after that.

A Legend of Sinukuan

A YOUTH from Magalang, Pampanga, was on his way to
his father's clearing at the foot of Mount Arayat one
afternoon when there came to him two softly whistled
reed notes quite unlike what he had ever heard before.
He looked in the underbrush and up among the
branches of the trees, but all he saw was leaves and
stems. "I thought I knew this place," he muttered half-
amused.

The whistled notes came again, and this time from
right beside the trail. He tiptoed after it and the
whistling continued. Following the sweet sound, he
advanced deeper and deeper into the woods, walking as
though spellbound.

At last he came to some wild shrubbery. And there,
in marked contrast to the overhang of vines that all but
concealed the trunks of the trees, stood a beautiful
maiden. She had the height of a village girl, but her
skin was unusually fair, her untrimmed hair wavy and
dark, her white gown long, loose, and sheer. A sheaf of
talahib reeds lay at her feet.

In a voice half-speech and half-whistled music, she
said, "I am Mariang Sinukuan, and I imagine you are a
youth from a village near by."

The youth nodded, tongue-tied.

"Come," she said, beckoning to him.

He hesitated apprehensively.

"Fear not, youth," she reassured him, and gesturing to the bundle of reeds at her feet, she added, "Sit down."

He did so, and the bundle lifted him off the ground, and the next moment he found himself in the hollow of a huge tree—or a tree he thought it was, but that same instant he realized that she had ushered him into a majestic dwelling place, clean and airy and well furnished with rich hangings of gold. In the center of the hall stood a table laden with food and good cheer for the travel-weary.

The maiden welcomed him to what she said was her father's home and asked him to partake of the food and drink.

But the youth had learned to be wary of taking food from unexpected sources. He had no doubt now, besides, that she was Mariang Sinukuan, and he had often been told that whoever partook of her food would fall under her spell.

"Thank you very much, but I am not hungry," he said.

"Not even a bite?" she insisted.

"I had something filling to eat before I came here," he replied, firmly making his head.

She let him go but made him vow he would never marry in his youth.

He kept his word, and many a maiden was to sigh in frustration because he never made good his promises of love to them. Only when streaks of grey flecked his temples did he marry.

It was told that Mariang Sinukuan's father was a bearded ancient sometimes seen leaning on a bamboo cane and shuffling up and down solitary trails on Mount Arayat. He had two other daughters, it was said, and they were as fair as Mariang Sinukuan, with hair as long and dark, noses as exquisitely shaped, and lips as luscious. Like her, too, they were just above five feet tall, had the dreamy eyes of a tropic afternoon, and were clad in long white gowns.

Three town youths were wayfaring along the slopes of the mountain one day when they met Old Sinukuan near a large, dark-leaved tree. On an arching branch of the tree his three comely daughters sat.

The old man smiled at the three youths and said, "Join us, boys."

They did so, for they were not familiar with local lore. The old man made them sit on a bundle of talahib. This raised them quickly aloft and bore them through the air. The bundle put them down at the foot of a big white rock and there stood other maidens as fair as Sinukuan's daughters, and with them the men who had fallen under their spell for incautiously eating the repast the maidens had offered them.

The three youths were offered food and drink, too, but they said they had had too much to eat and drink at the fiesta before they came up on the mountain for a better view of the village.

Failing to cast a spell on them, Old Sinukuan made the sheaf of grass take them back to where he found them.

It is still told in the towns and villages around Mount Arayat that Sinukuan's daughters may be seen at the outskirts of the mountain or on the streets, market places, and even the town squares. It is said that speaking in sweetly whistled notes, they try to entice unwary youths into their realm and hold them there forever.

The Desired One

ONLY TWELVE or thirteen, shy at first but easy of smile in due time, she had been for the entire year an errand girl in the household of a school supervisor in Romblon.

One afternoon she complained of a throbbing headache. A headache pill was given to her and she was advised to go to bed. She was up early the next morning and was at school all day. But about sundown when she came home with the other children her headache was back.

Another pill gave her relief for the night, but the next afternoon it was as before. Her severe headache returned promptly after the angelus bell rang.

So when her parents came down for a visit, bringing gifts of edible shoots, hornbill mushrooms, wild honey, and eggs from woods birds, the supervisor suggested that she be shown to a doctor. But her father, who was by way of an herb healer, demurred. "She has *atipuyong*," he said, "a headache that comes when the sun rises or when it goes down. Or maybe she has *malaot*, the result of an encounter with a harmful spirit."

It turned out that it was more nearly like the latter.

As a healer he was unusually communicative about his vocation and explained that this daughter's case was not worth the expense and trouble of a consultation with a trained doctor. He placed a few burning charcoals in a coconut shell and then cast some garlic kernels, ginger peelings, feather, and a few herbs on the coals. He had the girl wrapped in a sheet, told her to sit on a chair, and put the shell brazier under that so the emanation rose to her. He also placed a handful of medicinal herbs on her head to cure the persistent aching there.

"This is *tu-ob*," he explained. "and it shoos the harmful spirits away. It is performed late in the afternoon when the spirits are abroad, much as a log is kept smouldering near cattle in the yard at night to keep the mosquitoes off them."

If anything, the effect of her father's medication was not clearcut. Now she had a headache and now she didn't, but it had to be admitted that on the whole she saw some improvement.

Then toward August she started talking about three good-looking strangers. They bore the unusual names of Cesare, Grimare, and Emare, she said, and had often asked her to pay a visit to their realm. They were each about five feet six, not a little taller than the average young men of the town. They had ochre skin like the neighbors but the thing that most arrested her besides their good looks was the levelness of their upper lips, which lacked the depression there known as the philtrum. She admitted without undue modesty that

Cesare, the handsomest of the three, had proposed marriage to her.

Now after each sunset she would make preparations for her unseen visitors from the otherworld. She would start eating of invisible food that she said they had given her as a gift. The visits from them lasted from thirty minutes to an hour, and during each visit she would become entirely unaware of the other members of her master's household. Her eyes would be half-closed as if she suddenly faced the light of noon.

More important, however, she would grow exceedingly strong and willful during those moments when the youths were visiting with her. She would attempt to get down from the house through the doors and windows and, these being bolted, through any small openings in the sidings and floor. She would declare quite frankly that she was eloping with her lover. The district supervisor and his sons had great difficulty holding her down then, and subdued at last, she would scream that her friends from never-neverland had left her.

After each fit she would suddenly grow shy and fagged out. She would just take a few disdainful bites by way of supper, evidently sickened with the taste of human fare. She would remark that she had plenty of food which her friends had left with her, though she refused to show or describe the food.

Not long after, about five in the afternoon, she was missed. A concerted search was made in the town and beyond, a search accompanied by much hollering of men and the yowling of dogs and the beating of sticks. At last she was found on a low hill some distance from the encircling delta. She was seated on a large rock under an old strangling fig. She resisted all attempts to lead her peacefully home and the menfolk had to all but drag her away.

Another healer, a woman, came and declared that the girl was under the power of an *engkanto*. "He insists he will marry her," she said.

She asked the girl if she had eaten anything her suitor had offered her and she shook her head. "But there stood a large table laden with food and fruit," she added, her eyes lighting up. "In the center of the table stood two big trays of rice, one of white rice and the other of black," she added. She also reported, a smile of delightful recollection breaking out on her lips, that Cesare, Emare, and Grimare showed her around their splendid mansion and she said the place glowed with the shimmer of gold and ornaments of precious stone. The walls glittered and the furniture shone like gold.

Because she refused to eat with them, the engkanto folk were about to start supper by themselves when she was wafted away and then found herself sitting on the rock where the townspeople found her.

"I'm glad you did not taste the black rice," said the healer. "If you had you would have had to marry Cesare. Then you would have died to us and gone to live among the engkanto of the strangling fig."

On the girl's bodice the healer pinned a piece of newly-dug ginger the size of her thumb so that the engkanto could not get near her again.

By September of that year she had fully recovered and her folks came for her and took her back to her village. She got over her ailment in due time and seems to be a normal, healthy village belle today, courted by and not unresponsive to the attentions of the village youths. She has never again been molested by the spirits of the trees.

Woman Elf by a Tree

PITONG RAN out to the fields and flew his kite near a tree that stood by a brook, The kite rose to the sky and the sun painted its wings a light red. It sat as still as a sleepy old woman in a corner up in the sky.

By and by the breeze rose and a sudden gust blew over. The kite pointed its nose to the ground, dived, and got itself caught in a branch of a tree.

Now the tree was a *bangar* and was the favorite home of elves. People never walked by the tree for fear of offending the elves there. The ground under the tree was always swept clean, it was said, by the elves living in the tree.

But Pitong said he did not believe in elves or any other creature he had never seen. He climbed into the tree and then, stepping on a branch to reach out for his kite, he heard a little cry of pain. *"Aray! Araay!"* it said.

He saw too late that he had stepped on an old woman about three spans tall. She had long, copper-colored hair, long nails, and a wrinkled—if fair—skin. She was eating her supper of yellow roots and black rice when Pitong stepped on her.

She scratched him and bit him and spat on him, but Pitong fought her back. Her nails and teeth were sharp, however, and at last he leaped to the ground and ran home shouting for help.

He lay in bed with a high fever all night. Before
sunpeep, his father went to call for an old woman who
lived alone in a grove at the outskirts of the village.
She clucked her tongue when she heard what had
happened. She ordered a white-feathered, white-legged
cockerel caught and then cooked it with soft white rice.
She put no salt or spices in the dish. She placed it all
in a bowl of polished coconut shell. Then she took the
shell to the foot of the elf tree at sun-dip and chanted:

> *Take this our toll*
> *For the harm our son did.*
> *Eat and forgive.*

By morning Pitong's fever had gone down and he
was soon at play again. But he never flew his kite near
the elf tree after that.

The Palasekan and the Phonograph

DURING their long study period after supper, the boys in a lonely farm school in the Ilongot country tried hard to stay awake. Even the teacher who was there to see that they stayed awake sat nodding beside the shiny phonograph in a corner.

Three soft, clear whistles like a trio of voices came from the darkness.

The boys looked up from their books and glanced through the open window. They had heard that the *palasekan*, elves from the deep woods, spoke to people in whistles.

Nobody stirred. By and by the whistling, clear and musical, came again. One of the boys pushed back his chair, rose, and announced: "The palasekan are talking to you, sir."

"What do the palasekan want?" asked the teacher. He always became a little cross when his nap was interrupted.

The boy glanced at the phonograph. "They say they would like to hear the phonograph," he said.

"Tell the palasekan that Mrs. Gabat is in town and has the key to the phonograph," replied the teacher.

The boy walked to the window and announced, "I am sorry, sirs, but Mr. Gabat says Mrs. Gabat has the key to the phonograph and is in town."

From the darkness the whistled reply came promptly. The boy turned back to the teacher and said: "The palasekan say Mrs. Gabat left the key behind."

"Maybe she did, but I don't know where she left it," snapped Mr. Gabat.

The boy turned to the open window again and reported: "Mr. Gabat doesn't know where Mrs. Gabat left the key, sirs."

The whistled reply came louder and in a higher key, as if in annoyance. The boy reported: "The palasekan say that Mrs. Gabat gave the key to the teacher and that the teacher put it at the bottom of the rattan suitcase under his bed."

Still the teacher did not want to play the phonograph. He was rather strict about study periods and believe that the phonograph needed a little rest. "We have lots of studying to do tonight," he said. "Tell the palasekan to wait till Friday evening."

The boy relayed the words to the darkness, and the palasekan snapped back with their whistled reply. "The

palasekan say that if the teacher doesn't want to play
the phonograph, they will play it themselves," the boy
said.

Then there was another whistle, just as sharp, and
the boy said: "The palasekan say the teacher may be
sorry later."

Reluctantly, Mr. Gabat rose. He pulled his bunch of
keys from his pocket and walked to his bed. He pulled
a rattan suitcase from under the bed, opened the
suitcase, and fumbled among the clothes and papers
there. In a moment he fished out a tiny key. He
walked over to the phonograph and inserted the key
into a hole in it and pushed up its top. Then he
cranked the phonograph and put on a black record.

For a good part of the evening, till the boys were
ready to go to bed, sweet, cool music came from the
loudspeaker that stood like a kangkong flower on top of
the phonograph.

Then there was a brief whistle, and the boy
reported: "The palasekan say thank you, sir."

Music in the Air

CARLOS and two other youths, his weekend guests from Manila, were one late afternoon walking to the former's country place in Lucena. Some fifty meters from the house they heard the blithesome strains from a string orchestra.

"Mother has probably invited friends to a welcome party," remarked Carlos.

"That's not necessary," replied one of the guests.

"But these provincial orchestras can sure play," remarked the other.

The tune, extremely moving and reminiscent of grain fields on a quiet afternoon, floated over to them.

Then, just as they crossed the gate, the music was gone.

"Very good, very good," the guests said.

They entered the door and Carlos called, but only a woman's voice met them.

Carlos announced that he had two guests with him. "Where's the orchestra, Mother?" he asked.

"In a minute," she replied from the kitchen.

"But where's the orchestra?" Carlos repeated.

"What's all this about, Carlos?" she replied, coming out of the kitchen and smiling.

So the youths told her about the music. "All three of us heard it, too," they said. "It was all very clear and moving and then it suddenly stopped."

"You heard it, too, then," she remarked. Nodding, she looked toward a big tree beyond the back wall. "So you heard it," she repeated.

"Tell us about it," said the guests.

She spread the cloth on the table and started to set supper. "They live up in the tree beyond the wall," she said. "We all think it's a tree, but those with faith know it's the home of the little folk. What those wanting in belief think to be fireflies are their light, what most think is the chirp of crickets is their music. What most people think are vines clambering up the trees are their stairways, and what most think are the branches are their ramparts."

"Tell us more," said the guests, charmed by her whimsy.

"Well," she went on, "to those they entice into their mansion they offer a choice between brown rice and white rice. Refuse the brown rice and take the white,

but if you must taste their rice, mind to squeeze
kalamansi juice on it. The grains will wriggle, for they
are worms. The wee folk offer it to him whom they
would like to be one of them. Then woe will be his, for
he must be under their spell forever and marry an elf
maiden who before he weds her will be beautiful but
after the marriage will grow black like a wrinkled duhat
nine days fallen from the bunch."

Many years later Carlos, now the medical director of
a hospital in Lucena City, heard a scholarly paper read
about mythical beings. After the reading Carlos
accosted the lecturer and related the incident of many
years before. "I'm a medical doctor and should not
believe what my mother said," he remarked rather
diffidently. "I have been trained to look at things from
a scientific standpoint, but I fail to see a scientific
explanation for the phenomenon witnessed."

The lecturer said he was afraid he could advance no
explanation either. "Fortunately," he added chuckling,
"my role as a folklorist is only to take down and report
on what the folk believe, not to prove or disprove it.
But lest I seem to be dodging my responsibility to
science, I must add that it was probably a case of
hallucination. For hallucination can be auditory,
olfactory, or tactile as well as visual. But since I know
that many who suffer from hallucinations end up in
mental derangement, I should hesitate to say that this
was a hallucination."

"A neat way to sidestep the issue," remarked a
psychologist, advancing toward the guest speaker. "I
believe it was an auditory stimulus just the same."

"But four of us heard it," objected the M.D.

"Forty could have heard it," replied the
psychologist.

A physics major cleared his throat. "What do you
think of this?" he volunteered. "There's such a thing as
air resonance. We all know that the air moves about.
You say, doctor, that your home was only a few
kilometers from town. On a stream of air, the music

must have floated in from a real string orchestra in the town. The music was probably carried to you and your guests by the breeze."

"I'm sure we heard it, at any rate," said the medical doctor.

"Then the wind shifted its direction and you thought the music stopped."

The folklorist nodded and so did the medical doctor, adding: "Thank you. I had some physics in college but I never thought of that angle."

He told his aged mother that explanation, but she pursed her lips, shook her head, and stamped her foot impatiently. "I still think it was music from the woods spirits," she sighed.

It is hard to say whether she said that because she believed in environmental spirits or she said it because she found it a far more satisfying explanation than the scientific one.

And who can blame her?

Letters from and to Frank

THROUGH A SLOPE of woods in Eastern Samar, Gloria and two other girls walked from their village to town each morning and back again in the afternoon, a distance of three kilometers. Seventeen and high school seniors, they were all pretty, but Gloria was the prettiest, graceful in her walk and a tinkle in her voice when she spoke.

One morning they found a pink linen envelope on a rock under a tree. It was their habit to stop under the tree and comb their hair before they entered the town. The letter was addressed to Gloria. With a titter she tore it open, pulled out a matching pink sheet of paper, and read:

Dearest Gloria:
    You are beautiful. Please be mine.

Lovingly yours,
Frank

The girls had heard of no one by the name of Frank, and they thought that the letter was just a prank. Gloria put the letter in its envelope and tucked it between the pages of her book and then the three walked on to school.

Gloria's friends thought it might be fun to return the joke, and Gloria thought so, too. So in the library they composed a reply together, and it went this way:

Dear Frank:
     But I have never met you.

Gloria

They left the letter on the rock on their way home in the afternoon.

A pink envelope lay on the rock the following morning, and the letter in it said:

Gloria dearest:
     Of course I will be very happy to meet you. Just tell me where.

Forever yours,
Frank

The three friends composed another letter, and it went:

Dear Frank:
     Drop in at home whenever you like.

Sincerely,
Gloria

They placed the letter in an envelope and left it on the rock on their way home. It was Friday and Gloria sighed saying this would be the last of the letters.

Promptly at midnight, she was awakened by the voice of her brother. "Gloria, Gloria," the voice said. "Open the door." With his friends he had gone out serenading earlier in the evening and now he had come home, or so Gloria thought, lighting a kerosene lamp and opening the door.

In stepped a tall stranger whom she had never seen before. His complexion was fair, his hair was wavy and yellow like corn tassels, and his eyes were gray.

93

He was the best-looking man she had ever seen out of
the movies in town.

"Who are you, and what brings you here?" she
asked, though in her heart she knew who he was.

"I am Frank. You asked me to come whenever I
like," she replied.

Then Gloria gasped, for the next instant he had
vanished.

Next day Gloria's parents found her talking to
herself. They did not let her go to school the following
week and sent for the herb healer. He observed her,
sadly clicked his tongue, and said that it was not to
herself she talked but to an invisible lover.

Gloria's friends felt quite remorseful because what
they thought an innocent prank had thrown their poor
friend's mind off course. They told her parents and the
healer about the letters, and the healer nodded and said:

"Her lover is a *dalakitnon*—an elf living in the *dalakit*
tree. She asked him to come and see her. He did, and
now she can never escape from his spell."

Gloria never recovered her mental balance. She was
dead in a year, and then it was said that her dalakitnon
lover had taken her to his world among the dark trees.

Ghouls

A Legend Grandmother Heard

FROM A SAILBOAT a youth from Batangas landed on a southern island and, heaving a big bundle to his shoulder, walked about the streets, shouting: "Mosquito nets! Beautiful mosquito nets!"

He made a few sales and then had his supper at a small eating joint. He walked about in the town some more and finally stopped at a big old house. He put his bundle down, cleared his throat, and said, "A man, sirs!"

Three pretty maidens opened the door. "Come right in, sir," they said with friendly smiles.

He shook his head and stroked his nape bashfully.

"Could you direct a stranger to where he might find a lodging for the night?" he asked. He did not think their parents and kin would lodge him.

The maidens smiled again. "There are other houses in town," one of them said. "But we will be glad to let you have our parents' room. They happen to be in the provincial capital for the weekend."

The bashful youth insisted that they should not bother. But they opened the street windows and smiled so sweetly that he found himself walking up the steps with his bundle.

It was time for late supper and they asked what they could offer him. He shook his head and said, "I

have had supper, thank you. Just go ahead and have
yours." He could not help noting how much alike they
looked and wondered if they were identical triplets.

"You are sure now?" another maiden said.

"We have plenty of food ready for guests on the
road!" put in the third maiden.

"You must be tired. Get some more to eat with us,"
added the first.

The youth firmly shook his head. "All I ask is a
place to lie down, thank you," he said.

They showed him into a room in the back, and he
was so tired that he went to sleep at once.

Later he was awakened by the smells of cooking.
He lay still and wondered why they resumed their
cooking so soon after he went to bed. From the sounds
of the night, he figured it was just past midnight. He
kept quiet trying to get back to sleep, but he soon heard
the maidens talking among themselves.

"Mine the left member," said one.

"Mine the right," said another.

"And mine the heart and liver," said a third.

They grew silent for a moment while they tasted
their dish, and then one of them said: "How tender!
He probably never worked in his life!"

Then he heard the second say, "Oh! We forgot we
have a guest in the house!"

"No matter," the third replied. "He is sound asleep
after a hard day."

But the youth heard it all and knew they were flesh-
eating ghouls. He quietly got up and pulled the sheet
over his pillow to make the bed appear as if he still
slept underneath. Then he climbed out of the window
and ran.

He returned next morning after he had had breakfast where he had his supper the night before. "Thank
you for a peaceful night," he told them. "I left before
you waked up."

"You're going to have breakfast with us this
morning," the first girl said.

"You must be hungry," put in the second.

"There is plenty to eat in the kitchen," added the
third.

The youth shook his head. "I have eaten, thank
you," he said. Then he picked up his bundle and left
as deliberately as he could. But he fairly ran as soon as
he turned the corner.

Perto and the Ghoul

PERTO'S OLD FATHER was ill and it was believed that a ghoul—a corpse-eating aswang—had been visiting him by night. Those who sat watching over him after dark whispered that they sometimes sensed an unpleasant smell coming from under the floor. And hadn't the dogs in the neighborhood been howling too often and too long of late?

One night Perto took off his clothes and covered his body with mud from the river bottom. "What's the use of my being the champion wrestler in the village," thought he, "If I dare not wrestle with the creature that wants to hasten my father's death so that it may eat him?"

He hoisted himself to the floor joist under his father's bed and quietly hung there. Before long the dogs raised their muzzles and started howling. Then a dark creature came out of the shadows and clung to the joist right beside Perto.

The night was dark and Perto could not make out the creature's appearance. But it had abundant hair, was bulky, and smelled like decaying flesh.

"Have you been here long?" the creature whispered in Perto's ear. Its breath indeed smelled like rotten flesh.

"I just came," Perto replied in a whisper.

"This man is stubborn," the creature added. "He has smelled like a ripe jackfruit for three nights and I thought he would die soon. But he continues to live."

"My father is stubborn and is not going to die yet," Perto thought. Swiftly he let go of the floor joist and grabbed the creature.

It clawed him, bit him, and kicked him. But the champion wrestler did not let himself be beaten. He worked his way to the back of the creature and held its neck with the crook of his arm. He gripped its wrists with his strong hand, reached for an abaca rope, and tied the creature to a post. Then he cleaned himself up in the river, put on his clothes, and quietly walked back to bed.

The villagers came out of their homes early at dawn and asked one another if they, too, had heard the heavy breathing and tumbling in the neighborhood about midnight. They hurried to the sick man's house and saw the pretty, wealthy spinster who lived in the outskirts of the village tied to a post with strong abaca rope.

She implored them to spare her life and promised to pay for the sick man's cure. They asked what made her molest the old man, and she told them her sad story. She was the youngest of seven daughters. Her ailing old mother could not die because none of her sisters would agree to swallow the black chick that lived in their mother's stomach.

Pitying her mother, she put her open mouth close to hers. Then out of the sick woman's mouth popped a feathered little black creature and dived into the daughter's mouth. "I have not been the same ever since," she added.

She begged the villagers to help her get the chick out of her stomach. She had them pile straw and sticks at the foot of a tree, tie her feet together, and hang her upside down over the pile. Then she had them kindle the straw and stick with an ember.

The smoke from the fire billowed up and she inhaled it and chocked. Near death, she retched and opened her mouth, and a fluffy black creature the size of a child's fist dropped into the fire. It had burned beyond recognition before they could pull it out of the fire.

Then they quickly took her down and untied her feet.

She lived as honestly as her neighbors from then on, and no one ever complained about her again.

Under the House of the Dead

A WIFE was having birth pangs one dark night and her husband hurried out to call a midwife. The rain began to fall on the way, he followed the amber glow of an oil lamp and came to a house in a grove.

He paused below the eaves, for it was well past midnight and he hesitated about waking up the tenants of the house. He had not stood there long before he heard a woman groan. He was glad he had not asked to be let in, for he would have hated to disturb her. He crept under the house and sat on his haunches to wait for the rain to pass.

In a little while the air grew heavy with a fetid smell. He looked around but could see no one in the dark.

Then someone came close to him and whispered, "Have you clung to the joist yet?"

The man did not know what the stranger meant, but he was frightened by the smell of rotten flesh the stranger exuded. He nudged the creature toward a beam of light that filtered through a hole in the mat and looked at his face.

The stranger quickly ducked back into the darkness, but one glimpse was enough. The creature had a hideous face, fierce eyes, a high-bridged nose, and long incisors.

The man's first impulse was to run. But he thought better of it, for the creature was likely to chase him and tear him up with its sharp teeth. If he stayed, the creature might attack him, too, but there was a good chance that it would consider him a friend and leave him alone.

"I said have you clung to the floor joist yet?" the creature repeated in a whisper.

"No, I haven't," the man whispered back. "I have just come."

Then the creature held on to two bamboo joists under the sick woman's sleeping mat, hauled himself up, and inhaled deep through the mat as if to relish the fragrance of her dying.

In a moment the woman made a groan more plaintive than before, whimpered, and grew still.

Then the creature came down and whispered in the man's ear, "It's your turn."

The man obediently took hold of the joists and pulled himself up. But his bones were thick and his muscles heavy and the joists creaked.

The dead woman's husband heard the creaking sound and rushed out with his glittering battle knife. He chased the creature while the man hid behind the stump of a coconut tree.

The widower came back cursing that he had lost the corpse-eating ghoul and then entered the house to guard the body of his poor wife against further attack.

Then the frightened man crept out of his hiding place and proceeded to call the midwife who lived beyond the rice fields.

Giants

The Origin of Mount Arayat

LONG AGO a giant named Ararayat lived in Northern Zambales. One day he scooped up some soil with his large hands from the shore just east of what is now the town of Candelaria. He carried the soil to the chain of islands southeast of where he lived. He stood on the highest island and saw a wide sea to the east.

Geologists—or scientists who study the physical
nature and history of the earth, including the structure
and development of its crust, the composition of its
interior, the types of rocks, and the forms of life—tell us
that a great many years ago the Central Luzon Plain
was a sea. This sea stretched between two chains of
islands that were to become the Sierra Madre in the east
and the Zambales Mountains in the west. A man could
have sailed back and forth on a boat from the Manila
area in the south through the Central Luzon Sea east of
the Zambales Islands—now Mountains—and on the way
to Lingayen Gulf in the north. Erosion slowly filled
that ancient inland sea with soil until the Central Luzon
Plain, now the rice granary of the Philippines, was
formed.

Ararayat walked to the top of the Zambales Islands—with the earth in his hands. Then he walked
down to the other side and dropped the soil in a pile in
the middle of the sea just north of what is now the
Candaba Swamp in Pampanga.

That pile of earth is still there and is now known as
Mount Arayat, the solitary mountain in the wide Central Luzon Plain.

People say that large depressions shaped like human
footprints can be found in the mountains above Barrio
Poonbato just east of the town of Palauig, south of
Candelaria. Similar depressions in the shape of footprints found in mountains and hills in various parts of
the world today are also said to be the footprints of
giants that once populated the earth but have since
disappeared, perhaps killed off by the warlike little
people who now rule the world.

The Stupid Giantess

FIVE LITTLE BOYS in the Cordillera country snared a wild boar deep in the green woods one day and killed it. The boar was so large that they decided to clean it and cut it into smaller pieces. Then they would find it easier to carry the meat home.

Under a tree by a lake they piled up dry sticks to build a fire to singe the hair of the boar. Then they found that they had forgotten their flint stone to start fire with. So they tied the boar to the branch of a tree and went to look for fire.

They walked this way and that way until they came to a big house. They crept in and found nobody there but a large fireplace with three rocks on it standing in a corner of the house. In the stove some embers still glowed.

The boys snatched an ember, put it in a nest of dry leaves, and ran back to where they had hung up the boar.

The big giantess Bekat, whose home the big house was, arrived after they left. Her nose quivered like a dog's as she sniffed about. She lowered her head to the floor and sniffed some more. Down the ladder and on to the lake she followed the boys' scent.

Coming upon them before they could flee, she said, "Let me divide the pig for you, my pretties."

They gave the boar to her and she tore it apart with her bare hands. She kept most of the meat and gave them only a fistful of the lean, saying, "Take this. The rest will be mine in payment for my fire."

The boys were angry but said, "What about a diving contest before you go, Bekat? If you stay under the water longer than any of us, we will gladly give you our portion of the meat, too."

"I better hurry home," replied Bekat. "I have something nice to boil in my pot."

"We will take just one dive together and then the contest is over," they said.

So Bekat agreed. The boys inhaled deep and dived, and Bekat inhaled deep and dived, too. Then the boys quickly rose to the surface, piled smooth, reddish stones from the lake, and hid the meat under a shrub. Then they climbed to the top of the tree.

At last Bekat rose to the surface, blowing water from her mouth and nose. She found the boys nowhere. She thought they were still under the water and had beaten her in the contest. Into her big burden basket she put the stones the boys had gathered and hurried away.

When she reached home, she poured the stones into her big black pot and its bottom fell off. "Those naughty boys have played a trick on me," she said. She tucked an axe to her waist and set out to look for them.

Reaching the tree by the lake, she smelled around for them like a dog but saw no one. She sat down under the tree wondering where they had gone. Then she looked into the water again and she saw their reflection there.

"There you are, you naughties," she said. "Now you will be sorry for tricking me." So saying, she dived into the water to catch them.

Of course she did not find them there. She dived in many times but did not find them. After she came out of the water one last time and rested, their image appeared there as soon as the water grew still.

Soon she had dived so many times that she felt like sneezing. She raised her nose and saw the boys high up in the tree laughing at her. "Let me see you try to escape now," she said with a big laugh. She pulled her axe from her waist and raised it to chop down the tree. "This tree will fall into the water and you will certainly drown," she said.

But the boys said, "Let Bekat cut her own knee," and she did.

Then Bekat aimed her axe at them, but the boys said, "Let Bekat cut off her own head."

Sure enough, the axe flew out of her hand and cut off her head, and that was the end of her.

Af erjo{I(

The Merman

SOLANG WAS PRETTY but she was near thirty and a man was still to come and claim her.

She and her mother walked to the river with the week's wash one morning. At the edge of the water they soaked the clothes in a basin, rubbed a cake of soap on the clothes till suds billowed over, and spread them out on the pebbled bank to bleach.

Then they bathed, soaping their long hair with thin lye from burnt rice straw. Solang's mother dried her hair and lay down for a nap in the cool shade. But Solang went on paddling about, splashing water on the bleaching clothes from time to time to keep them steaming.

After a while she thought she heard someone call her by name. She lifted her eyes and looked, and there, waist-deep in the river, stood a man.

"What are you doing here, Uncle Asiong?" she asked. She turned to tell her mother, but she was still asleep. Then she looked back at her uncle and her jaw fell, for he had become a smiling youth, his handsome neck, shoulders, and arms gleaming dark copper in the morning sun.

"Come here," said the stranger.

"I will! I will!" Solang exclaimed with a giggle.

"Are you talking to me?" her mother asked, propping up her head with one hand.

"No, Mother," replied Solang.

"I thought I heard you speak," her mother said.

"But not to you," she said a little impatiently. "I was talking to him." She gestured toward the handsome youth but he, too, was gone.

Solang's mother rose quickly and waded to where Solang stood in the water. "Are you all right, Daughter?" she asked anxiously.

"Uncle Asiong was in the middle of the stream a moment ago," Solang explained. "Then he was gone and a young man stood there."

"You are tired," her mother said.

"I'm perfectly all right, Mother," Solang replied.

They beat the clothes on the flat crown of a gray rock that stood out of the water, rinsed them, and laid them out to dry. Under the tree they ate their lunch of rice and roasted fish wrapped in banana leaves. They sat down to let their lunch settle, and then they picked up the clothes and walked back to the village.

Solang's father fetched an old widow who helped the ailing with muttered chants and made offerings to the creatures of the dark with whom, it was said, she had secret dealings. Solang's mother told her what had happened at the river and the widow nodded. "What your daughter saw," she said, "was an *ugkoy*, a merman, who wants her for his wife."

Murmuring secret words, the widow burned some guava leaves and chicken feathers in a little clay brazier, and she made Solang inhale the heavy smoke from these. Solang slowly calmed down and was soon asleep.

Departing, the widow said the ugkoy could not bear the smoke and had left. The girl's parents breathed easier.

But early next morning they discovered that Solang was missing. She was neither in her room nor in the yard, and she was not at the village store. They traced her footprints to the river and there, on the same spot where they had been the day before, she stood earnestly talking to no one. They asked her what she was about and she replied that the youth had come for her at dawn and had insisted that she go to his underwater realm with him. Her face had a strange glow as she talked, and there was a mirthless smile on her lips and a wild light in her eyes. She even capered on the water like a dancing girl.

They took her home against her will. She could not get to sleep but made fishlike motions on her sleeping mat. "Water, water!" she said. "How wonderful to be in the water with your man!"

The old widow and Solang's parents burned more guava leaves and feathers. They added *subusob* leaves, lemon grass, and human hair on the burning coals for good measure. They burned these all night under the house and beside Solang's sleeping mat where she lay.

But she never got over what she insisted she saw. She grew more restless and more haggard each day, and then she seemed to hear no other voice but that of her merman lover.

One morning her parents awoke to find her gone. With their neighbors they followed the prints of her feet to the river. She was not there, and they followed the winding stream to where it joined the sea.

She lay floating face down in the salty water, and she moved every which way the waves moved. Her long hair pointed in all directions like the leaves of a seaweed, and her arms were stretched out as if she had leaped forward to embrace her lover.

"She followed her merman," the old widow healer said with a sigh, "and he refused to take her all the way to his realm."

The Boy Who Dived Too Deep

THREE BOYS, Apron, Mimoy, and Senen, did not walk straight home from school one afternoon but detoured to the sea. There they stripped and agreed to have a diving contest. He who stayed in the water the longest would win.

Apron and Mimoy soon surfaced. They waited for Senen with mounting anxiety, but as he did not reappear, they knew he had drowned. They put on their clothes and ran home to tell his parents.

The villagers swarmed out to the sea and the strong men dived in search of Senen, but failed to find him. They stopped searching only when night

came. Then they returned to the village and mourned over him.

Meanwhile, Senen had dived so deep that he came to where myriads of bright fish were at play. He pursued them till he reached the bottom of the sea. There the water suddenly clouded and he fainted.

When he opened his eyes, he found himself lying in a soft bed. A pretty mermaid sat smiling beside his bed. She said she was queen of the deep and had long been looking for a boy who should become her king when he grew up. "At last I have found you," she added happily.

"But I cannot be king," Senen protested. "I am not a prince. I am a mere village boy, and you must send me home because my folks will be looking for me."

The mermaid smiled again. "Forget your folks," she said. "You will be my king." Then she had her mermaid servants bring in food on golden platters. "This will help you forget," she said, offering the food to him.

He shook his head vigorously and did not take any of the food, for he had been warned against accepting food from strangers.

The mermaid smiled and said, "If you won't, then don't."

She led him around her palace and showed him the shining jewels on the floors, ceilings, and walls. Senen had never imagined such a magnificent palace any-where. There were painted fish and bright sea flowers in the gardens, too, and the rocks enclosing the grounds were covered with all sorts of pretty growing things.

Then the mermaid tried to feed him again, but he refused to eat.

The days went by and he became thin and weak. He thought constantly of his parents, his brothers, and his sisters and playmates. He remembered his teacher smiling before the schoolhouse under the trees each morning.

One day at noon the mermaid took him out for a swim. They stopped where the sandy road forked and she said, "I have wanted very much to keep you in my realm, but you refuse to stay and become my prince. You have grown pitifully thin and weak when I want you to be healthy and never die. I brought you here so you can make your final choice." Then she pointed to one road and said, "This road leads back to your village. Take it if you really want to return to your people."

Senen followed the road with his eyes and saw it covered with sharp stones. It went up and down and then disappeared in the distance.

Then the mermaid pointed to the other road. "This road is smooth and gentle," she said. "It swings around and then comes right back to my palace. It is smooth, and your feet will not get hurt as you walk on it." She looked at him sadly and added, "I cannot keep you in my realm any longer because you refuse to eat. You are free to choose. Take the rough road and return to your village where you will grow up into a common farmer and marry a common girl. Or take the smooth road back to my palace and grow up into a prince who will be king of the sea."

Senen followed the rough road with his eyes again. It was narrow and bumpy all the way, but it swung up to the upper world where his village and his people were. Then with his glance he traced the smooth wide road. It swung around through beautiful underwater gardens and then came back to the mermaid's palace. It was bordered with gems and precious stones, and it ran smooth all the way.

Finally Senen looked at the mermaid again and said, "Thank you for saving my life and letting me see your wonderful world. I am sorry but I don't belong here. My folks and friends are waiting for me in my village."

He turned and left, and the mermaid wept as he disappeared.

The Woman Under
A Merman's Power

NICANORA had been wed to a sailor who had been
away for many years. He had promised to come home
after the third year. When the three years were up, he
had written that he would not be home till after three
more years. But now eighteen years and a war had
gone by but he was still away.

One morning Nicanora told her mother that for a
month now she had been hearing the voice of a man
asking her to go to the sea with him. She confessed
that she was much worried because she could hear the
voice but could see no speaker. She could get no sleep
and the color in her cheek faded. She would be startled
when spoken to no matter how softly, and then she
would weep and weep.

An *herbolario* came to look her over and said that a
merman had her under his spell. If she was not
watched, she might one day be found floating in the
water too late for rescue. Before the herbolario left, he
let her inhale the fumes from burning onion and garlic
flakes.

But the sorcery of the merman's calls did not sub-
side. Nicanora said she could see her handsome lover
waving from the river and she shouted back, "Yes, yes,
I'm coming." Then she hurried down the ladder, but
her brothers held her back and put her back in bed.

Her parents took her to the hospital and there the doctors found her blood pressure too low. They gave her shots in the arm for a week, but she did not get any help from that either. She kept on hearing the voice of her merman lover.

The village priest said a prayer for her and sprinkled holy water over her and around the house. This eased her mind somewhat and sent her into a profound sleep. But she awoke next morning with a start as usual, saying, "I come! I come!" Only by force was she restrained from running off to the river.

A woman herb healer next came and looked her over, and she wondered if they would let her ask the tree elves to drive off the merman who had her under his power. On a shallow basket the medicine woman placed some cooked pork, glutinous rice, cane wine, and cigars rolled out of leaves from the midsection of a tobacco plant. Then at starpeep she laid the offering in the elf-tree. As she did so she danced and chanted entreaties to the spirits in the trees to rid Nicanora from the merman's spell.

Having done this, she chewed betel leaves with shell lime and a few areca nut cubes. Then she rubbed the mash on Nicanora's body and murmured her to sleep.

Next day, Nicanora woke up, and she was her usual sunny self. Never again did she hear the voice of her merman lover, and though her husband never came back and was eventually listed among those who had been lost in the war, she never lost her mental balance again.

The woman herb healer got full credit for the cure, but since recovery from an ailment such as Nicanora's takes plenty of time, no one could really tell if it was the woman herb healer's ministrations, the priest's, the herbolario's, the physician's, or the recuperating powers of her own body that should be given credit for her recovery.

Werebeasts

The Weredog and the Boy

A LITTLE BOY awoke before cockcrow and cried, "I am hungry. I am hungry!"

"Be quiet," said his widowed mother. "We'll wait till the day breaks and then we will go buy bibingka when the widow Kulli has baked some."

"I can't wait!" said the boy. "Go get me some cold rice and a piece of sugar loaf."

The mother picked up the oil lamp from the stool and walked to the kitchen. She reached up to a bamboo frame hanging from the rooftree and brought down a clay pot and a lump of brown sugar. While she was paddling out a chunk of red rice that had caked hard in the pot overnight, the boy screamed that he was hungry.

"Yes, yes, I'm coming," said the widow, putting back the pot and sugar on the frame and hurrying to him.

As she entered, she was horrified to see two blue eyes aglow in the dark. The lamp light showed a big black dog, its fangs shiny and sharp, and the creature was attacking her son.

She ran behind the door and whipped out a ray's tail tucked there. Then she rushed to the monster and whacked at it.

Yelping in pain, the monster leaped out through the window, its bushy tail tucked between its long legs, and vanished in the dark.

The eye of suspicion fell on the men on a road construction crew in the village. Three of them spoke Tagalog with an accent that showed they were from the islands farther south. They had been suspected by the other workers to be out for mischief rather than for pay, but it was impossible to say for sure.

When the crew had moved out of the village some weeks later, their work done, the foreman was heard to admit that one of his men had left weeks before, his back lacerated with three ugly welts. "I would not be surprised if he never came back," the foreman was reported as saying.

The little boy's wounds were severe and it took months and much tending to get them healed. But from then on, he knew better than to shout and send his mother off with the oil lamp to get him food in the dead of night.

In the Werebeast's Den

TWO LITTLE BROTHERS in Argao, Cebu, were playing outside Old Imo's yard one afternoon. They became thirsty and wondered aloud where they could get water to drink.

"Right in here, my boys," said Old Imo, suddenly appearing at his window. "The water in my jar is cool and sweet. Come right in."

They went into the old man's house and had each a
good drink of water. They thanked him and said they
were going back to play but the old man brought out
some rice cakes and told them to eat. Then he brought
out toys for them to play with.

They ate the cakes and played with the toys, and
night had fallen when they remembered they ought to
be home to help their mothers with the evening chores.
But Old Imo said it was dark and they should not be
out because werebeasts were liable to smell them out
and get them. "Why not spend the night with me?" he
added. "Your parents will be happy to see you in the
morning and glad you did not get lost after all."

The boys had enjoyed playing with the toys and
were indeed loath to go, so they played on.

Soon the man had cooked supper and bade them
eat. After a while, following their good supper, they
felt drowsy. The old man put them to bed on a smooth
sleeping mat of fragrant reeds in the inner room and
himself lay down at the door.

Later in the night, the older boy was awakened by the scraping of a blade on a stone. He lay quiet and listened closer to make sure. The scraping went on. The boy rose quietly and put his eye to a slit in the nipa wall through which the orange glow of an oil lamp filtered.

There he saw Old Imo crouched over an oilstone and sharpening a knife. The blade gleamed briefly in his hand as he paused, brushed his fingertips across the cutting edge, and muttered with satisfaction, "There's tender meat tonight. There's tender meat for eating tonight."

The boy turned and shook his brother. "Shh! Let's get out of here!" he whispered.

"It's still dark," mumbled the other, sitting up.

"I say let's get out of here," repeated the older boy.

"But I'm very sleepy."

"Get up, I tell you!" the older boy was frantic. He pulled his brother up, shoved him quietly out of the window, and climbed out after him. Then they ran home.

They told their story to their parents and got a spanking from their mother for staying out late and a heavier thrashing from their father for sleeping in a stranger's house instead of bringing in home the carabaos from the fields and feeding the chickens.

Witches

The Woman with the Lizard's Eyes

IN THE OUTSKIRTS of a remote village in Leyte there once lived a widow named Igay and she had two daughters. Igay's face was remarkably plain and she dropped her gaze quickly when spoken to. Those who succeeded in looking into her eyes said that the pupils stood upright and thin like the pupils in a lizard's eyes.

She had found herself a husband who was quite friendly and far better favored than she. The folks liked him and sometimes wondered how a man and a woman so unlike each other could have married at all. One day the two had a terrible quarrel. The man's abdomen was seen to swell soon after and he died in agony. Then word got around that Igay was an *osikan,* a witch.

The two daughters were shy like their mother but were fair and had the likeable ways of their father. Two young men came to claim them at a tender age and they were married in the same year.

But not long after, the belly of one and then that of the other young husband swelled, and both died in close succession. The folk said they had displeased their mother-in-law and she had filled their bellies with noxious bugs and snails and killed them by slow death.

From then on the village folk avoided Igay and her daughters like the pox, and they had to move to an-

other village. There they found an empty hut under a
bamboo grove beyond the line of houses. They lived all
by themselves, fishing in the river with sieves, gathering
lentils from the river banks, and avoiding and being
avoided by the villagers.

In time the story of how Igay's husband and those
of her two daughters died caught up with them. Soon
they had to move on to the next village. There they
received the same cold stares and had to move on. This
went on until they reached our village.

None of us knew who they were, of course, but
before long Igay was being called an osikan. It was
said that she was a *paburot* besides, a witch who could
make people swell and burst. If she said "Ondo will
grow big," the body of Ondo or whoever she named
would grow enormous and he would soon die.

A farmer's daughter was having her noon meal in
her father's field at harvest one day when Igay came
walking by. Courteously the girl said, "Come and have
lunch with me, Aunt."

"No, thank you," replied Igay. "Just go on eating and then you will grow big."

In a day or two the poor girl's belly started to swell. She was in great distress and lay on her sleeping mat contorted with pain. She was dead in a week and an uncommonly large coffin had to be made for her, so big her belly had grown.

The menfolk of the village had known the girl as a sweet little maid. With fire in their eyes, they sharpened some slender bamboo into spears. Then they marched to the hut where Igay and her two daughters lived.

The three were at their meal and the men set upon the old witch. But she suddenly became an ugly bird, flapped its wings, and fluttered out of the window. The bird sailed to the top of a big tree and screwed its beady eyes around to look at the frightened girls screaming for mercy below.

The men hurled their spears at the bird, but it flew into the woods. They followed it and surprised it drinking at a spring. Then an unerring spear hit it in the breast and the bird fell with a terrible squawk.

The men cut the bird to pieces and scattered the pieces on both sides of the stream into which the waters of the spring emptied. "That way," they said, "the pieces cannot join together, for a witch is afraid to cross a body of water."

They never saw Igay or the likes of her again. As for her daughters, the people let them live on in the village. In time they found new husbands and lived happily with them and their neighbors.

The Men Who Went
to a Funeral

KIKAY, the prettiest maiden in the village, had many suitors, but she accepted Sintong, the farmer's quiet, hardworking son. Rodolfo, the son of a wealthy man from an adjoining province, saw her at the village fiesta and fell in love with her. Through her parents he sent Kikay many gifts as a token of his intentions, and through her parents she let him know that she had given her heart to Sintong and could give it to no one else.

Rodolfo and his gifts stopped coming, and then Kikay started to suffer from a fever that would not abate in spite of the ministrations of the herb doctors. It was then, too, that she began acting funny.

It was rumored that Rodolfo had been seen at the hut of Narda, the witch, and the villagers nodded to one another knowingly.

Kikay's parents took her to the provincial hospital and she stayed there three months. But she did not show any sign of recovery and was brought back home. On the way home she sang with a blank stare, and it was noted that her voice had become high-pitched and was sweeter than her former voice. Some recognized the voice as the witch Narda's, and word got around that the witch had indeed taken possessions of her and was slowly sapping her vitality.

So Kikay's parents sought the help of a *manggaga-mod*, a medium known to be able to counter the ailments inflicted by the *mangkukulam*. The manggagamod tried her occult powers of medication, but she finally admitted to the girl's parents that the bane which the witch had inflicted on Kikay had taken too deep root because her folks had been slow about taking Kikay to her. She predicted that at the girl's funeral, Rodolfo, her frustrated suitor, would come to exult over his victory.

Kikay soon died, and sure enough, among the many who appeared at her burial was Rodolfo, who had paid her no visit in all the months she lay ill. He came in a red car with his cigar-smoking father.

Seeing the two, Kikay's indignant relatives rushed upon them both with bludgeons and bladed weapons, and when the dust cleared, Rodolfo and his father had been dragged out of their car, all bumps and bruises, and their clothes torn off. Even prompt attention from the doctors failed to save their lives.

Duel Over a Bellyache

A LITTLE BOY of ten had been writhing from a severe stomachache for an entire week. So his father crossed a two-piece bamboo foot bridge over a creek to call Selo, the old medium.

Selo came, asked a few questions, put his hand on the boy's abdomen, and said, "There is an egg in here."

The boy's parents had thought so, too, and were glad Selo confirmed their suspicions. The mother recalled that Tasia, the balut vendor, had sold a few half-hatched duck's eggs to her a week before and she had not liked the look on the vendor's face when she asked her to replace one egg that had a crack on its side.

Was Tasia the woman who never looked one in the eye when spoken to?

The parents nodded.

That woman was a witch, truly.

Tasia and her husband lived beyond the last row of houses in the village at the far side of a plateau right next to the mountains. They were without a plot of ground to till and lived by gleaning in the fields after the farmers had gathered their crops. They also lived by fishing and by trapping snipe and quail.

The boy's father pulled out a bamboo spear he kept hidden behind the granary door and strode to Tasia's

hut. He found her in her yard, dragged her out, and
threatened to ram the spear through her chest if she
failed to take the egg out of his son's belly.

Was he saying that she had put an egg in the boy's
abdomen?

And he was saying that she must take it out right
away or else he would kill her.

But she had done no such thing and so would not
know how to get the egg out.

Tasia's husband came home from his fishing just
then. A fierce bolo duel followed and both men cut
each other up. The neighbors came and carried them
on stretchers to town for treatment.

The doctor who attended to them heard their story
and sent for the sick boy. He felt his belly, gave him a
few red tablets, and told him to stick around.

In about an hour a big ball of intestinal worms that
had formed in his belly was expelled. "So the egg
became worms!" exclaimed the neighbors.

The doctor shook his head. "It was worms, not a
witch," he said and turned to dress the wounds of the
two men who had fought over the belief in witches.

The Naughty Girl and the Peddler

SOME FRIENDS of Aurora's invited her to a fiesta in Taguig, Rizal. At the final bus stop a wizened old balut peddler addressed her: "Buy some balut from me, my pretty. This balut is nice and white like your complexion. Surely, one so beautiful must have loads of suitors."

Aurora looked at him over her nose and said, "What business is it of yours about my complexion and suitors? You're just a balut peddler!"

He returned her proud stare as her friends led her away to their host's residence.

Aurora and the other city guests were enjoying the heavy fiesta luncheon at the balcony when she saw the same peddler glaring at her from outside the gate. He caught her eye, turned, and was gone.

Aurora soon felt something not right with her and told her host so. She and her friends boarded the bus back home ahead of the other guests.

She began acting oddly from then on. She did not seem to know what she was about. She avoided visitors and stayed in her room. She who had been outgoing was suddenly bashful.

"Are you well, Daughter?" her parents asked her. "You have to tell us so we will know what to do."

"I'm all right," she replied.

They gasped, for her voice was that of a total
stranger's. "Say that again, Daughter," said her father,
but she clammed up.

She sat down on a chair and her feet, which had
been those of the lanky girl that she was, failed to reach
the floor. This surprised them, too. They made discreet
inquiries around and it was suggested that someone
was in possession of her.

She was no better the following week, and then her
parents took her to a medical doctor. The doctor
looked her over and plied her and her folks with questions. He said she should stay in bed and return after a
day or two if she did not feel better then.

Her folks were not particularly impressed with the
consultation and sent for an herb healer. He came and
looked Aurora straight in the eye. Then he nodded
gravely, turned to her father, and said, "You daughter
has been witched."

"I thought so. But by whom?"

"That we will find out," replied the healer. "But
first promise not to interfere with or comment on my

cure if you want your daughter to get well." He took a
broom of coconut-leaf ribs, whispered a spell, and
touched her arm with the tip of the broom.

The touch made her recoil in terror and in a male
voice wailed, "Stop it! Stop it!"

"I don't intend to stop it," replied the healer sternly.

"Stop it, Master, I beg you! Stop it!" repeated the
voice through Aurora's lips. "You are killing me!"

"I will kill you," said the healer. "unless you leave
Aurora."

"I will leave, Lord!" said the voice.

"Don't promise. Just leave."

The healer stopped plying her with the broom and
Aurora quieted down and soon fell asleep.

"If I know them," muttered the healer to Aurora's
parents as he turned to go, "he will come back. Send
me word if she acts funny again."

And sure enough, in the afternoon Aurora suddenly
got up, plainly not herself.

The healer came, more stern than before. "Now you
will get the torture you more than deserve," he said in

a level voice. He brought a chicken feather out of a
kerchief he had in his pocket, whispered a secret spell,
and inserted it between two of Aurora's toes.

Then the familiar male voice issued from Aurora's
lips. "My toes will break!" it exclaimed.

"That serves you right for being stubborn," said the
healer.

"I can never walk again!" cried the voice as the
healer brushed Aurora's feet with the feather.

"You will die if you don't leave," said the healer.
Again he brushed Aurora's feet with the feather, and
the wails from Aurora's lips grew in accents of agony.

"I am leaving!" said the voice at last.

"Go ahead, leave!"

"I am leaving, I am leaving!" said the voice, and it
trailed off like a wail from across a river and then still
fainter like a call from over a hill.

Aurora stood up as if she had never been ill. She
saw the people in the house and asked in a voice now
hers. "What goes on here so early in the morning?"

The people looked at one another knowingly and let
her go back to sleep.

Never again was she naughty even to impertinent
peddlers.

Why We Go to Folk Healers

A MAN in a small provincial town had gnawing pains in his belly. He groaned and twisted but did not send for the healer because he wanted to try the government hospital in Manila. Over his transistor radio he had heard that part of the taxes he paid went to the salaries of the hospital staff, and he thought he should get help from them.

He put on his canvas shoes and with his wife took the first bus to the city well before cockcrow. From the bus terminal two hours later they inquired around and were guided to a street where they then took a jeep to the hospital. They entered the hospital grounds and, by inquiring some more, found the public dispensary.

A notice at the door said the staff would be in at nine. The clock with the luminous face said they must wait and so the couple sat down on a bench.

Other patients shuffled into the dispensary and sat on the benches. The patients compared their illnesses and from the way he felt, the man from the small town was sure he needed the most urgent attention.

At nine no staff had arrived. At nine fifteen the door into the staff cage opened and an attendant sauntered in yawning. He was followed shortly by a nurse who was checking on the whiteness of her shoes. She was followed by another nurse who began to compare her short hemline with that of the first nurse. None of the three even glanced at the patients who now filled the seats.

At nine-thirty the attendant opened the window at the dispensary counter. Our man who came from far away through woods and fields was conducted to the counter by his wife but the attendant waved them back to their seats saying the doctor had not yet arrived.

The couple retraced their steps to their bench and waited some more. As slowly as he could he counted ten and waited. All the time he was bent with the pain and his wife kept on wiping the cold sweat off his brow. At eleven there was still no doctor. Unable to bear anymore the man stood up, gave the staff a baleful look and left.

Ogres

The Children and the Buso

THE RICE CROP was ripening. Clouds of red sparrows flocked into the kaingin to eat the grain, and the farmer told his two little children, a boy and a girl, to go and drive them off.

The children walked to the middle of the clearing. They sat in a little shed there and shooed off the birds with pebbles.

By and by a gruff voice came from a large tree at the far end of the clearing. "Just wait till I finish my new burden basket," the voice said.

"Did you hear that?" the girl asked her brother.

"It's but the wind in the trees," said the boy.

They sat on in the shed driving off the birds, and soon they felt drowsy and dozed off.

Then a *buso* came down from its tree. It had a big new burden basket on its back. The children heard its heavy footsteps, but when they opened their eyes, it was too late to run. The buso had but one eye and it glittered in the middle of its forehead. It had sharp teeth, and a shiny red horn stood on its head. It was an ogre—a cannibal giant.

The buso turned its back to them, sat down, and said in a big voice, "Be nice children and comb my hair."

The children combed his hair and pulled out ugly black worms and lice. They were sickened at the sight and said, "Your hair is clean now, sir."

Then the buso put the little boy and girl in its burden basket and stood up saying, "Up we go."

From out the basket the girl cried, "Wait, sir. My comb dropped into the grass. Let me just get it."

The buso sat down again and let her climb out of the basket. "Be quick about it," said the buso. "I'm hungry and there will be tender meat for dinner in the big tree tonight."

The girl quickly picked up a big stone and handed it to her brother in the basket. Then she picked up another and gave them to her brother, who quietly put them and another in the basket.

When there were enough stones in the basket, the boy climbed out. Then the two children quickly hid in the rice plants and the girl said, "I've found my comb, sir. We can go now."

The buso rose and walked straight home while the children quickly climbed up into a tall betel nut tree.

The buso climbed into its tree and said to its wife, "Cook these. We'll have tender meat for dinner."

But when it poured the contents of the basket into its wife's cooking pot, the bottom of the pot dropped off and the stones rolled out to the floor. Its wife laughed and said, "Your tender meat is hard enough to knock out the bottom of my pot."

Out the buso rushed in a rage, sniffing this way and that till it came to the *mama-an* tree. It looked up into the tree and saw the two children there. "There you are!" it said, licking its lips. "It's not too late to cook dinner yet."

The mama-an was too thin and tall to carry the buso, and the buso could not climb the tree. But a little *bagkang* tree grew at the foot of the mama-an. The buso saw the bagkang and said, "Now I'll pry you children loose." Then it added:

> "Up, up, bagkang;
> "Down, down, mama-an!"

The bagkang started shooting toward the top of the
mama-an, and the mama-an began growing down to
meet it. The children did not know what to do. Soon
the bagkang reached them. The buso started to pry
them loose from the *mama-an,* and the little girl
screamed with fright.

Quickly the boy picked some nuts from the mama-
an. He threw the nuts at the top of the bagkang and
said:

> "Down, down, bagkang;
> "Up, up, mama-an!"

The bagkang grew down and the mama-an grew up.
The children breathed freely again, but the *buso* said:

> "Up, up, bagkang;
> "Down, down, mama-an!"

The bagkang started to shoot up again and the
mama-an began growing down. Soon the buso was
trying to pry them off the mama-an, making the girl
scream louder than before.

But the boy picked some nuts and threw them at the
bagkang with these words:

> "Down, down, bagkang;
> "Up, up, mama-an!"

Again the bagkang grew shorter and the *mama-an*
became as tall as before. This went on and on. At last
the buso grew tired and walked home. Then the children climbed down the mama-an and ran home.

From that time on, their father planted no rice in the
clearing near the big tree of the buso.

The Fisherman's Wife and the Ogre

A FISHERMAN and his wife lived in a little hut between a river and a dark jungle. He left her one night to go fishing. "I will be home before sunrise, Wife," he said. "Bolt the door and windows tight."

"And take good care of yourself," she replied at the door.

A *busaw* stood in the shadows and heard them. As soon as the man was gone, it made itself look just like him, walked to the foot of the ladder, and said in the voice of her husband, "Wife, I am home early. Let me in."

She sniffed through a hole in the door and knew from his strong smell there that this was not her husband. She quickly took her comb and whispered, "O my faithful comb, there is a busaw out there in the yard and he wants to eat me. Tell him I have fled to my father's house. Tell him to come another time."

The busaw rapped on the ladder and said, in her husband's voice, "Wife, do you hear me? I have come home early. Open the door and let me in."

Then said the comb, "O busaw, my mistress is not here. She is in her father's house. Come another time."

The busaw believed what the comb had said and stalked back into the shadows.

"Thank you, O my faithful comb," said she, putting the comb back on her hair

Early next morning the fisherman came home with plenty of fish in his basket. He found his wife still trembling with fear in a corner of the house and asked her, "What makes you tremble so, Wife? Here's plenty of fish for your cooking."

"The busaw came after you left," she replied. "He pretended he was you and wanted to come in."

The man never again left his wife alone by night, and he let a sharp bolo hang down through the bamboo floor to keep the busaw safely away.

Vampires

Waders in the Night

MISS SIMANGAN, a young teacher from the north country, had been with the provincial high school in the central islands for almost a year. One day she joined a fellow teacher, Miss Elamparo, to spend a weekend in Bay-ang, the latter's village.

The road was tortuous and bumpy. When the two teachers got there, the church bell was ringing out the Angelus. The guest was tired but was sufficiently awake to note that Bay-ang was just a few scattered nipa houses in a grove of old trees.

She also noted that the faces of those who met them, Miss Elamparo's parents among them, were rather tightly drawn and their eyes a bit on the large side. But she felt that the people's mouth hygiene was efficient, something a young school teacher was bound to notice, for their teeth were in perfect shape.

At supper the two teachers had a hearty appetite after their long journey. They particularly enjoyed the *dinuguan*, sliced pork cooked with blood and a favorite of most Filipinos, to be sure. Miss Simangan found herself harboring a feeling, though, that dinuguan have been perfect if there were just a pinch more of salt, bay leaf, and cinnamon in it.

The two vacationists went to sleep directly after supper, so tired they were after the long trip and, Miss

Simangan admitted to herself, they had eaten too much.

Miss Simangan was awakened by distant quacks in the middle of the night, but she did not mind, for Bayang was far from traveled roads and close, she imagined, to a swampy area. It had been long since she heard the calls of night birds, and the calls added depth to the silence of the rural night.

She could not get to sleep for quite a while after she awoke, and dark thoughts bothered her and gave her a hint of how outmoded beliefs about maleficent creatures of the night originated among the unlettered.

She eventually floated off to sleep but was awakened not long after by the flapping of wings. She slipped off her gold ring and quietly placed it on Miss Elamparo's finger. Next she took off her watch and put it on her companion's wrist. Then she tiptoed to the other side of Miss Elamparo, lay down, and pulled the sheet over herself.

In a moment two creatures fluttered into the room, tiptoed over, and fastened their teeth with tiny shrieks of delight on her poor friend's neck. Terrified and in a profuse sweat, Miss Simangan nevertheless lay quiet.

Poor Miss Elamparo was stiff and cold at cockcrow, and Miss Simangan walked out, hurried to the *tartanilla* stop, and anxiously waited for the first tartanilla run out of the village.

Two Strangers

IT WAS EVENING in a sleepy old town on the foothills of
the Ilocos range when a girl with a striking figure
arrived at the shed where several young men were
sipping cane wine. She spoke from the rig which she
came on and gave her name as Josefa. She said she
was from the South, but since they did not know what
that meant, they did not ask her just where in the South
it was.

All her wordly possessions were contained in a
rattan case. She said she did not wish to bother anyone
about a place to lodge in now but wondered if there
was an empty house where she could stop for the night.

Several houses were mentioned and she chose one at
the edge of the town right next to the hills. She admitted it was not quite proper for a woman to put up
alone in a strange house at night, but she asked the rig
driver to take her there anyway. Three of the boys
gallantly led the driver to the place. She carried her
case up the old steps, thanked the boys, and said she
would look for a place nearer the town square in the
morning.

That night, the boys clustered under the eaves of the
house and filled the neighborhood with the strains of
songs to her. She appeared briefly at a window,
thanked them, and bolted the doors and windows tight.

She came to the wine store next day and said she kind of liked the house and wondered who owned it. She was told that the owners, a childless old couple, had died some months back. So she decided that she might as well stay on in the house.

In the next few days the boys visited her one after another and declared they loved her. She smiled each time but shook her head and said she was too young to be thinking of such things. The boys did not think her answer satisfactory, so they kept coming back.

Within a month, three of the healthiest young men in the town, but not among those known to have called on her, died in their sleep. The people were puzzled somewhat, for three healthy young men had never died in one month before.

A stranger came to town in a knock-kneed old rig one night. He was good-looking and, told about the pretty stranger, proceeded to her abode for a visit.

"He is her husband and has come for her," some said after he left.

"He is her suitor and they will marry," said others.

"They are evil folk and their coming to our town is not for our good," said an old woman.

People who next day quietly walked by the old house and looked from the corner of their eyes wondered why the two strangers had not come out of the house. The doors and windows were still closed.

They waited till late the following day and then made their presence known by clearing their throats at the front steps. No one opened the door and so they forced their way in.

They found the two locked in a tight embrace. The tip of the long tongue of each planted in the neck of the other. Then the people knew they were vampires who had sucked out each other's blood dry during the night.

Viscera Takers

The Squid Child

A WOMAN IN POTOTAN, Iloilo, had her first baby after much pain, but it did not look much of a boy or girl. It looked more like a squid, with its dark, glassy eyes, two frail tentacles for arms, and two deformed end flippers for legs. Elderly folk who came to look at it left sad-faced and muttering that when it was a fetus it was *na-aswang*—sipped all but dry of body juices by a viscera sucker.

Asked if she knew when it all happened, the poor mother told them that one night her husband had left her alone in the house to go fishing out in the bay. She sat making clothes for her coming baby, and when she

looked up she saw something thin and red like an over-extended earthworm cascading down from the roof. Wondering, she brushed the worm off with a broom and it withdrew.

But in a moment it came billowing right down to her again. She screamed with all her might then, and the neighbors came running and found her all by herself.

"Do not ever again go night fishing," she begged her husband when he came home at sunpeep, and he promised.

But a week later as he was coming home from the village wine shed, his head addled by fumes from fermented palm juice, he saw a dark form on the ridge of the roof. He knew what it was and quietly climbed up a steep ladder to it.

"You got up here ahead," he whispered. "Your first visit?"

"My second," replied the creature. "I was here last week and then went elsewhere for my food drink."

In a flash the husband whipped out his spear from its sheath and jabbed it into the creature. It rolled down the roof and flew away, not dying because it healed its wound by licking it dry with its tongue as it flew.

The monster never returned. But it had done damage to the baby, and so it was born looking more mollusk than human, its legs like tail fins, its arms like tentacles, and its two eyes large and bulgy as if staring out of the deep.

The Smiling Sisters

A MAN from Camarines Norte married his high school sweetheart and they had four children. When he became forty he fell into the company of a woman from another town. She was long of limb and had a ready smile, and she had two equally comely sisters.

His wife soon found out why he stayed away from home so often. With the children she left him and went to live with her parents, and he too left to join the girl and her sisters. He had an easy life with them, and he had not a worry in the world. There was plenty of rice and meat in the cooking place, and the three pretty sisters made him feel that his company was all that mattered to them.

One night he reached out in the dark and found his mistress not on her side of the sleeping mat. He struck a match and looked but she was nowhere to be found. Her sisters were not in their sleeping place either. He waited at the head of the ladder wondering whether they had not gone out for a breath of fresh air, for truth to tell the night was warm. But a cockcrow passed, two cockcrows, and they did not return. He went back to bed and waited some more and then he was sound asleep.

At dawn when he woke up, he found the three
sisters making breakfast in the cooking place. He asked
where they had been and they said, "Just out for a
breath of air."

He went to bed early the next evening so that his
sleep would be light. There was no incident then nor
on the following night. But on the third night he
glimpsed three figures leaving through the window, and
reaching out for his bedmate he found that she had left.

He stayed in bed with his ear cocked against their
return, and before dawn he saw them slip back in.
Contrary to what he had heard told about women able
to go through the air unaided, they had no wings.

He cleared his throat and said, "Weren't you out a
little long?"

"You did not tell me."

"The fiesta was far," said the middle sister.

"We didn't want you to get cross," added the
youngest.

"Ask me to join you next time," he said.

Nothing happened for a week. He grew homesick
for his wife and the children and he went to visit them.
Once there he told her the truth between him and the
smiling woman and begged her to forgive him and
come back home with the children.

She forgave him and returned home.

Two weeks later he felt a finger poke at the small of
his back between two slats in the floor beneath the
sleeping mat. He rose and walked downstairs, carefully
balancing himself on his toes.

Over the landing the three sisters floated weightless
to him from the dark. "You said you wanted to come
along," they whispered, reaching for his hands.
"Come."

They lifted him up unresisting and let him through
the air like a little child learning to take his first steps.

Over the fields they floated, over the trees, and then
high over the salt sea beneath the blue and orange stars.
Beyond the sea a village with a few scattered lights
soon came into view. "There's the fiesta," they said.

"Yes, I see," he replied. "How did you know there
was a fiesta so far away?"

"The fragrance. It came across the sea." They
gently put him down on a mango tree and added: "We
won't be long."

They slanted toward a nearby house, but he climbed
to the ground and followed them behind a hedge of
reeds. He hid in a banana clump near the house and
watched unseen his three companions sitting on a
corpse while a mother and father moaned over their
dead.

Then he hurried back to the mango tree, only paus-
ing to pick an orange from an overarching branch on
his way.

The sisters soon returned and they took him by the
hands as before and headed for home with him. "You
are somewhat heavier," they said. "Did you pick up
something?"

"Only a fruit," he replied.

"Throw it away."

He dropped the orange and hurried home with no further trouble.

"I came down and saw you sit on the corpse," he told the eldest after they got home. "Why?"

"We savored its fragrance," she replied.

"I have heardit told that to some people, a pregnant woman smells like young rice roasted and pounded clean in a mortar," he said. "What does a corpse smell like on the bier?"

"Like a ripe jackfruit, of course," she replied, tittering at his ignorance.

"You should have let me come into the house, too," he remonstrated.

"Next time," she said, caressing him. "There will be many more fiestas."

They came back a week later. "Are you ready for the next fiesta?" they asked. "We'll let you come in with us this time."

"Not tonight," he replied.

"I don't feel well now, but I'll come to your home and try to get well there."

So they lifted him up as before and carried him to their home in the next town. As soon as they left, he entered a closet in the back of the house which he had never seen them enter. There he found their lower bodies standing side by side like fragments of wooden figures. He picked up the one at the left and put it in the middle and then he reversed the relative positions of the other two. Having done this, he hurried downstairs and hid in a bush.

Before long he heard the sisters' plaintive voices. "We can't tell, we can't tell," wailed the youngest.

"Which is whose and whose is which?" whimpered the next.

"Help, O gentle lover!" said his mistress.

But he kept still.

"The east brightens," cried the youngest, her voice failing.

"Soon the sun, and we will die," shrilled the middle sister.

"O lover sweet, help us!" pleaded his mistress.

He came out of the bush and climbed up into the house. He put their lower bodies back to where they had been, and then without trouble each of them joined her upper body to her lower.

"Did you bring me a coming-home gift?" he asked after they had thanked him.

"We were too long and came home not too soon," they replied, very sleepy.

They left again a week after and then, feeling about in the thatch inside the closet, he found three phials snugly tucked in behind a post. The phials were filled with oil such as he remembered hearing women like these dropped into the three holes under each of their armpits before they segmented themselves and took off. He put the phials in his pocket and went back to sleep.

A bundle lay at his side when he rose at sunup. He peeked into the bundle and saw chubby legs. He tiptoed out with the bundle tucked under his arm.

At the police station the desk sergeant raised his sleepy head, and his eyes popped when he saw what he had brought in. The man led the police team to the house where the three women still lay asleep. They handcuffed them and put them sleepy-eyed into the town jail, unable to fly because they had not put flight oil into holes in their armpits.

The man returned to his family, and never again had he to do with women too ready to smile.

A Viscera Sucker
at an American Base

IN THE EARLY DAYS, long before motor cars came roaring into the Olongapo naval base and you could still spear large eels from a rowboat in the clear waters of the river Kalaklan nearby, all the police officers at the base and even in the adjoining village for civilians were Americans.

A young mother sat fanning herself on a low stool one evening in May. She was alone because her husband was on the night shift at the drydock. Her first child was due in a month and she had been making diapers for several evenings.

A piece of thread, fine as hair, lightly touched her elbow and she brushed it off absent-mindedly. Then the thread touched her knee and it felt wet and she saw that it was pink. "I never had this color thread in my sewing basket—and why should it be wet?" she thought, snatching it. To her surprise the thread grew taut, like a fish line with a big dalag at the other end of it. The thread ran straight from her hand to a tiny hole up in the ridge of the nipa roof.

When the thread was so taut that it cut into her finger, she picked up her scissors and snipped it. There was a squawk from the roof and the long thread was swiftly withdrawn. The piece in her hand wriggled. She dropped it with a grimace and it lay writhing on the floor like a snake with its back broken. Then she heard a heavy object roll down from the roof and fall into the backyard with a thud.

She ran to the front window and shouted for help. The neighbors came with bamboo spears, bolos, and pistols. The first men to get there said they saw a feathered white creature flap awkwardly over the fence and flee like a gamecock beaten in a fight.

Others who came soon after said they met a tall American dressed in his police uniform stumbling off in a daze, his clothes stained with blood as if he had just been in a fight. And those who came still later said they saw the uniformed white man disappear moaning into a side street that led to the woods on the far side of the river.

"It was an American manananggal I am sure," said a white-haired old villager.

"An American viscera sucker, grandfather?" asked a youth. "That can never be."

"And why not?" replied the old man. "A man or woman can become a manananggal in any of three ways—by eating food touched by a manananggal, by eating food that the manananggal has partly eaten and wet with her spit, and by swallowing the chick that has lived in the dying manananggal's stomach and made her crave for human viscera all her life. So if any person does any of these things, he becomes a manananggal. It does not matter whether he or she is black, brown, red, yellow, white, or any combinations of these colors—and let me add that I know of enough combinations of these in this nice village of ours.

Sounds in the Night

A YOUNG WOMAN fresh from nursing school was assigned to the central islands and married a youth there. Her first baby was due in three months, and after supper it was the young couple's habit to stroll to the outskirts of the village. Her books said that an expectant mother who had walking exercise would have an easy delivery.

One night after they had gone to bed he woke her up. "Can you hear what I hear?" he whispered.

She listened but heard nothing. "I can't," she replied. "What is it?"

"Listen!" he hissed.

She listened again, and by and by she heard something. "It's just a house lizard," she said. "It caught a bug and is beating it against the thatch to stun it before swallowing it."

"You may be right," he said. "But I better patch up the roof in the morning."

She said he might as well. "The monsoon will be here in a few weeks, to be sure," she said.

Next day he patched up the saddle roof with scraps of discarded nipa shingles. But the following night he still heard the sound, and she agreed she did, too. So at bedtime next day he took a coconut bowl and filled it half full with a mixture of salt and vinegar and with mashed garlic, onion, and ginger. He put the bowl within easy reach and trimmed the oil lamp till it gave a bright glow.

At owlcry he was awakened by what seemed like pandanus leaves flapping in the air. Then he sensed that the sounds of flight stopped on the roof. A tiny hole then appeared in the roof ridge, and by the glow of the lamp he saw what looked like a long red twine. The twine began dropping toward the bed.

Quick as a lizard's tongue, the youth got up and reached for the bowl of spices. He tossed its contents to the roof and the air was filled with spice aroma.

At once the red twine withdrew and there followed a clatter of leaves. The youth unbolted the window and looked out just in time to see somethnig dark fluttering away toward the distant woods.

When it was morning again, the youth put a patch of tin along the ridge of the roof. Then he sharpened six bamboo ends and fitted them into pairs. He hoisted them to the roof and put each astraddle the ridge, spacing them evenly.

"That," he reassured his wife, "will keep the fetus-sucking creature at a safe distance from now on."

Stranger in the Night

MARIO, a youth from Cavite, was on his way home to his farm upon a night so quiet that the chirrity-chirr of crickets in the grass all but deafened him. He had just turned a crook in the path when he saw a human figure standing beside the way. He wondered why anyone should be there all by himself at such a time of the night. "Quite dark, isn't it, neighbor?" he said.

"Yes, quite," replied the stranger, coming over and getting into step with him. "I'm Berto. Do I know your name?"

Mario was certain he had never heard that voice before. "You are headed for the barrio, too?" he asked, deciding to give the stranger another chance to prove by the timbre of his voice that he was an acquaintance.

"Not really," was the reply. "I'm but a wayfarer and have no place to put up for the night."

Mario was pleased at his having been proved right about the stranger's voice. But he was naturaly soft-hearted and was moved by the latter's words. "I live all by myself," he said after some hesitation. "Would you like to spend the night under my humble roof?"

The stranger thanked him and said that he had been resigned to spending the night under the trees. "I'll be very happy to sleep under a roof after all," he said.

Soon arrived at Mario's hut, the two ate and Mario
gave his guest his new sleeping mat on the cot and himself
lay down to sleep on the floor.

There was much excitement at the town market when
Mario got there to buy his week's supplies next day. A
woman had been found disemboweled in her sleep. The
crime was without precedent in the place, and what most
shocked the townfolk was that she had been such a sweet
soul without a single enemy.

"This is no crime at all," one was saying, "if by a crime
is meant a human misdeed against another."

"It was no human being did it," put in another. "Her
guts are gone. Only an aswang could have done such an
evil thing."

Sure enough, at the autopsy, it was found that not
only were the victim's intestines gone but her heart, liver,
and lungs were missing, too.

Mario decided to drop in at the house of mourning
and took his guest along. The latter followed him up into
the house but chose to sit with the other callers at the
landing instead of advancing to the coffin to mutter a
silent prayer for the dead as was customary.

After they returned to the barrio. Berto said, "It's a
warm night."

"It's warm, yes," Mario replied.

"I want to go out for some fresh air. Would you like to
come along?"

"I've had a hard day behind the plow and need some
sleep," said Mario.

As soon as Berto left, Mario got up and trailed him,
slipping from shadow to shadow. He followed Berto into a
banana grove and there saw him disappear for a moment.
Then, trailing him with utmost precaution, he saw Berto,
in the half-light from the moon over the dark trees, the
upper half of his body slowly rising, taking on wings, and
flying away.

Mario tiptoed to where Berto had been and came
upon his lower section where it stood against a banana
tree. Mario moved the section a little to one side, sprinkled
salt on it, and sat in the shadows.

At the night's meridian the grove darkened and the flap of banana leaves in the wind increased. Then Berto's upper body came in over the trees, swung down to where the lower stood, and glanced past it wings a-clatter.

"You will have to try harder," Mario muttered to himself.

Again Berto flew past his lower body. He hovered over the latter but failed to join his segments together.

"Try again," Mario said aloud.

Berto then fluttered over to him and begged: "Wipe off the salt from my body friend, and push it back to where I left it. Unless you do so before the east lightens, I die."

"You will only go out and kill more helpless people if I do," replied Mario coldly.

"I vow never to do it again," said the monster. "Help me become one again and I will never be the monster I have been."

Mario meant to be hard on the creature but its pleas were so plaintive that he relented. He brushed off the salt with his sleeve and put the inert body back to its original position.

Then the upper body flew over, linked up with the lower, and in an instant Berto stood whole.

Berto was a good as his word. He was soon accepted as a member of the village community, acquired a little land of his own, and became a farmer. And he got over his peculiar ways of obtaining meat.

The Women of the Woods

NIGHT OVERTOOK a ten-man survey party in the woods of Panay and they decided to look for a likely shelter till morning. Coming to a clearing, they saw a house of bamboo and nipa under a large *bubog* tree. After briefly consulting among themselves and wondering how people could live so far from human neighbors, they crossed over to the gate.

An old woman met them and they asked if she had room for them just for the night. She said she did, she always provided for folk who were likely to get lost in these deep, dark woods, and would they please come in?

They asked if she lived all by herself so far from roads and trails.

No, she didn't, she had three daughters who, though the guests hadn't asked, were rather pretty. Unfortunately, they had had supper early and had gone to bed. "Just wait till I get you some supper yourselves," she added.

They said, "Thank you," but they had brought their own provisions. All they wanted was a place to cook, eat, and then stretch out their legs and get some sleep. And could they have a dash of salted fish or even just a pinch of salt? They had forgotten their supply at their last camp site.

She did not seem to have heard the last question and so they had a saltless supper.

After their meal, they tried to make conversation with their hostess, but she yawned three times, four times. They had done a lot of traveling that day and were a bit tired. So they distributed themselves on the floor, the head of one man side by side with the knee of the next so that five pairs of eyes were turned to each of the two windows of the house, one window at each side. Soon only the leader of the team remained awake and the other were breathing the deep, regular breath of people asleep.

Near midnight the leader of the group heard faint movements in the inner compartment where the old woman said her daughters slept. Out of the corner of his eye he saw a figure flutter to the left window, sail out, and disappear in the night, its long feathers hissing faintly. Next a second figure flew to the right window, shook its shoulders, and flapped out. Then a third figure flew to the left window and likewise fluttered into the night. When all three had left, there was an eerie stillness in the house.

Carefully the man crawled into the inner room. He groped about on a big sleeping mat there and made out a wide sheet spread over the mat. The sheet covered three slender forms stretched side by side, and by feeling over the forms he ascertained that they were the lower bodies of humans cut clean at the waist. Nothing lay between the waists and the pillows, which lay end to end, but one who might have merely glanced into the room could have thought nothing amiss, for the sheet was taut.

The man crept out to the fireplace where they had cooked supper and filled his fists with ashes. He tiptoed into the inner room and sprinkled the ashes over the cut portions of the three bodies. For good measure, he also took some pepper from a pouch he always carried on his waist and sprinkled it over the ashes.

Then he returned to his companions but did not go back to sleep.

Shortly before cockcrow he heard the flutter of wings, and the upper bodies of three women flew in, the first through the left window, the next through the right, and the third through the left again. The creatures dropped their individual bundles by the fireplace as they flew past. The man knew that these were human viscera which these *wakwak*, self-segmenting monsters of the night, had sucked out of their human prey through their elongated, tubelike tongues.

Having dropped their plunder, the creatures fluttered into their sleeping compartment, but they soon came out again, pleading: "Kind friends, may it please you to wash off the ashes and pepper on our lower bodies! Merciful

173

friends, we did you no harm while you rested in our home.
Do us no harm now!"

The rest of the men awoke now, too. Their leader
pulled out his knife, one useful for puncturing the throat of
a wild boar at bay, and said, "Monsters, unless you vow to
renounce your liking for human heart, liver, spleen, lungs,
intestines, and voided phlegm, we will leave you to die!"

"We so vow, we so vow, merciful friends," the creatures chorused.

"You must also vow to do useful work and never
harm people again," added the leader.

"We so vow, we so vow," they replied.

The old woman had awakened, too, and she added:
"Kind, merciful friends, they will become human from
now on if you will spare their lives."

So the men dashed water on the clean, oval sections
where the old woman's whelp had cut themselves in two.
Then each monster joined her upper body to her lower,
and at once they became pretty maidens.

The men hurried away, and it is said that the three
wakwak abjured their selfsectioning habits and can-
nibalistic appetite and became humans.

The Pretty Girl at the Cabaret

AT THE OUTSKIRTS of the town of Lilio, in Laguna, once stood a cabaret. After supper each evening men flocked to the ticket window, bought a fistful of twenty-centavo tickets each, and spent the rest of the night twirling, swaying, or trotting with the girls. Every three minutes the music ground to a stop and the males either clapped for an encore or walked their partners to their seats and surrendered one of the tickets to them.

There were many out-of-town belles in the cabaret. They were from various parts of the islands, but mostly from the Bicol provinces and the Visayas, as one could judge from their accents. Drawn to the cabaret, young men — and others no longer young — from Lilio and the neighboring towns were there night after night, especially after the harvest season.

Not far from the dance hall stood a low frame house of many rooms, and there the dancing girls were stabled, one or two to each room. Like owls they slept all day and emerged after supper, dressed up and painted to make their living.

Most comely among them all was a newcomer. She was known to have come from one or the other of the Camarines provinces, and many admiring eyes followed her graceful figure up and down the floor as she waltzed or slow-dragged or fox-trotted in the arms of the stags. She was closely watched because of her beauty, and one particular habit of hers became notable. Promptly at half past eleven each night when the moon was full or near full, she would excuse herself from whoever happened to be dancing with her at the moment and hurry home. But promptly at two o'clock she would be back dancing with the youths till four in the morning — the elder men had gone home earlier.

A young admirer, nephew to the dance-hall owner, was intrigued by her peculiar habit and decided to find out what she did at home during her two-and-a-half hour break. He could not believe that she left the cabaret to get herself some sleep and why only during those periods of the moon.

One night during the full moon, when she slipped out of the hall, he followed her, nimbly darting from shadow to shadow. He hid behind a clump of yearling palms and watched her enter the house. Then he crept up to her room and hunted for a peephole. He was met by a solid wooden siding but looked under the low floor. This was fenced off with a lattice of bamboo and he felt about until he found a

break in the lattice-work made big by the passage of stray
pigs.

He crawled on his belly through the hole.

The two-inch slats of flooring were nailed half an inch
apart for better ventilation and sanitation. What he saw in
the yellow light of an oil lamp through the slats confirmed
what he had heard told by elderly townsfolk in their tales
about comely strangers. The taxi-dancer stood in her
nighties. She reached up to a shelf for a phial, which sent a
brief flash of light in her hand. He knew at once from the
tales he had heard that the phial contained chicken
droppings in coconut oil.

She dipped her right forefinger in the phial and then,
with her oil-wet finger she drew a thin, deft line from the
outer side of her left little finger, just where the corner of
the nail met her skin, thence up her hand along the line
separating the skin of her palm from the back of her hand,
up her arms to her armpit, and down her side. Finally,
bending like a folk dancer, she dipped her finger into the
phial again and continued etching the line of oil down the
outer side of her leg till it reached the tip of her little toe.

Having done that, she next dipped her left forefinger
in the phial and drew an equivalent line on her right little
finger, hand, arm, side, and leg, thereby setting off the
front half of her body from the rear half. As she did this,
she muttered, softly but loud enough for him to hear: *"Siri,
siri! Daing Dios kung bangi! Labas sa kahuyan, lagbas sa
kasirungan!"* (Siri, siri! God is no night! Hence over the
woods, hence under the roofs!)

Then her anterior half, along with her entrails,
separated from the rest of her body and she surged out of
the window, floated over the trees, and was gone. The
cocks and hens uttered a suppressed cry of fear as she
soared over the branches they roosted in.

The youth was sickened by the discovery and ran
home in disgust and terror. He could not sleep that night
nor eat for two days. He told his uncle what he had seen

and the uncle let the pretty dancer go. But since then, the youth never again saw a woman of pleasing features but wondered if she, too, did not at night draw two parallel lines of oil and chicken droppings, first on one side of her body and then on the other, and flew out to forage on human entrails when the moon was gibbous or full.

A Flying Delegation

A WEEK-LONG seminar was held in Quezon Province during the summer break. Delegation from various towns in the province came to the seminar and were housed in separate school buildings in the town.

Last to arrive was an all-female delegation with unusually pleasing physical features. They came by night and asked to be billeted in the old school building at the center of the town.

This was easily arranged, for the other delegations had expressed preference for less antiquated quarters. The seminar organizers also thought it would be convenient that they be quartered near the police headquarters and be that much safer from molestation by the town's brash youths.

That night the townsfolk living near the central school heard the noise of wings and the *"Tik-tik-tik!"* of creatures in flight over the housetops. They felt not a little ill at ease, for they knew that the *tik-tik* bird was a scout for the viscera-taking aswang, said to be far when the calls of its scout were loud and near when the calls were faint.

The townsfolk bolted their windows tight and lay awake listening apprehensively. The braver men peeped through holes in their thatched walls and were horrified to see, limned against the full moon in the meridian of night, a flock of creatures sailing over on heavy dark wings, each topped with its round human head, erect and with long hair streaming behind like the tail of a comet. The creatures had no lower members, and then the folk were sure they were *manananggal*, monsters adept at segmenting themselves at the waist in the deep at night, leaving their lower bodies in their beds, and flying out to forage.

Word of the strange sights and sounds of the night quickly spread in the community next day, and the people assigned to give catering service to the out-ot-town delegates made discreet scrutiny of their guests. Those billeted in the central school were observed to be beautiful indeed but had peculiar food preferences. They steered clear of highly spiced dishes but made short work of meat and entrails cooked in pig blood. What they especially handered for was roasted ox heart, liver, lungs, and spleen. They were so fond of this dish that their hosts had to go shopping for these limited items in other towns in each morning of the seminar.

The armpits of these delegates were also observed to be unusually deep. "They need deep armpits," said some, "to tuck in the tiny caster of special oil they each need to propel themselves through the air." Added other folk: "And so the holes they inject the oil into while in flight cannot be seen."

The pretty delegates were red-eyed and some remarked that they were sleepy by day because they were up and about all night.

Crosses of pointed bamboo appeared on one rooftop after another, and bunched onions, garlic, and ginger were hung over each window in town.

There was a general sigh of recaptured peace in the locality when the closing remarks at the seminar had been made and the last delegation had left for home.

www.ingramcontent.com/pod-product-compliance
Lightning Source LLC
Chambersburg PA
CBHW050909260726
48660CB00001B/116